W9-COB-624

YOU TAKE JESUS, I'LL TAKE GOD
How To Refute Christian Missionaries

YOU
TAKE
JESUS,
I'LL TAKE GOD

How To Refute
Christian Missionaries

by Samuel Levine

HAMOROH PRESS
P. O. BOX 48862
LOS ANGELES, CA. 90048

**Hamoroh Press
Los Angeles, Ca.**

Copyright 1980 by Samuel Levine
All rights reserved.

Library of Congress Catalog No. 80-82731
ISBN 0-9604754-1-9 Paperback
ISBN 0-9604754-2-7 Hardcover

Printed in the United States of America

TABLE OF CONTENTS

Page

PREFACE

This book was written as a response to the many Jewish people that I have met who have either adopted Christianity or were seriously considering it. Since all of them, without exception, did not know the Bible or their Judaism before they were introduced to Christianity, they were easily manipulated by Christian missionaries (some of whom had converted from Judaism themselves). The purpose of this work, therefore, is to demonstrate the arguments used by the Christian missionaries, and to present a full presentation of the flaws of those arguments.

The first section of the book will discuss the most popular arguments and proofs used by Christian missionaries.

The second section of the book will be a presentation of some excellent questions which could, and should, be asked to any missionary, or to anyone seriously considering becoming a Christian. These questions point out the real defects of the Christian point of view.

The third section consists of an actual series of letters between a missionary and myself. You will see how the arguments are dealt with, and most important, you will get a feeling for the Christian mentality. This is especially true if you follow the discussion closely, and if you look up all the sources that are quoted. Once you know how a missionary argues, thinks and persuades, an actual confrontation with one will not fluster you at all.

INTRODUCTION

Before we begin our analysis of Christianity, there are a few important points to keep in mind.

The most important lesson that you should learn from this book is the *method* of dealing with Christian "proofs." It is not necessary to memorize the refutations that will be mentioned here. Instead, learn the method. Get the feel for what is happening, and after a while, try to refute the "proof" before you read my refutation. This book is simply an elaboration of a few key procedures which will enable anyone to see the inadequacy or falseness of any Christian "proof." Here are the procedures:

1. If they quote from the Old Testament, then
    a. Look at the entire context of that verse—usually this alone will suffice.
    b. See if the verse has been mistranslated—you should always try to look up every quote in the original Hebrew. If you do not know Hebrew, find a friend who does.
    c. See if the verse seems to be misinterpreted—see if the interpretation is forced into the words artificially.

    d. See if the verse points exclusively to Jesus; see if the verse could apply to another person as well.

2. If a Christian missionary solemnly warns you that you will burn in hell forever unless you accept Jesus, or if they try any other type of psychological trick, calmly ask them for logical proof for their beliefs. Insist on intellectual reasoning.

3. When missionaries present one of their proofs, and meet a question in return, they often do not answer the question. Instead, they usually throw another verse at the person. When this occurs, calmly insist that they answer the question that was asked.

4. Try to speak as calmly as you can. Jesus freaks believe that only faith in Jesus will make a person calm, and so your getting excited will only reinforce them.

5. Never be on the defensive. Be aware that you are most probably dealing with a brainwashed person, and not a rational theologian. There is therefore no reason to feel defensive or uncomfortable if you disagree with them. If they interrupt the discussion and ask you if it would be all right for them to immediately pray for your soul, do not let it faze you. That is a psychological trick that they use, and you might want to respond to it by singing a song or praying for their soul in return.

In addition to the above procedures, keep the following points in mind as you read this book. Whenever a verse will be quoted in this book, it will usually be from the King James Bible, with a slight change to make it slightly more modern. For example, "you" might be substituted for "ye." I chose the King James Bible since it seems to be the most respected, and so that you will see the verse as the Christian sees it. Furthermore, when a verse is quoted, it might seem to be in the wrong place, but only by one verse. For example, Deuteronomy 12:32 in the King James Bible is Deuteronomy 13:1 in the Jewish Bible. After reading this book, you should be able to discover the explanation for all of the discrepancies.

The abbreviations that will be used to refer to the books of the Bible will be the standard ones. The most frequent ones will be: Gen. (Genesis); Ex. (Exodus); Lev. (Leviticus); and Deut. (Deuteronomy).

It is also very important to remember that thirty terrible proofs do not prove anything at all. After reading this book, you may feel that even though each "proof" of theirs is not a proof at all, still, perhaps there is some truth to it. So remember, thirty or forty terrible proofs do not equal even one proof; $40 \times 0 = 0$.

In addition, realize that most people who accept Jesus into their lives did so for psychological reasons, and not because the verses of the Bible convinced them. Very often, if you probe deeply enough, you will discover a broken home, a terrible marriage, an unloved person—in short, someone who needs a Big Daddy to comfort them. Jesus fills that void for them. So realize that if you know someone about to accept Christianity, do not debate Christianity with him or her until you have had a long talk with them about their personal life. What they need is, most probably, a good friend, not a psychological father figure who will be placed on the wall with his hands stretched out on a cross. Usually, if you see that someone accepted Christianity without thoroughly analyzing the various "proofs," then there is a great probability that there is a personal problem in their lives. On the other hand, if you see a strong concern for the theology and the "proofs," then that person is probably interested in the truth. In that case, let him read this book immediately.

Furthermore, I would like to apologize for my use of the term, "the Old Testament." I am convinced that there is only one authentic "testament" from God, and that is the text known as the Torah. It happens to be the same thing as that which is called the Old Testament, but the word "old" is used to connote that which is replaceable, or that which was replaced. That is what the Christians mean when they say "the Old Testament," and that is why Jews resent that term. However, for the purpose of effective communication, it unfortunately must be used. Thus, you will find the word "Torah" used often, and other times, "Old Testament"; they mean the same thing.

Before we begin, there are two most crucial points to make. As we all know, any change in a status quo needs to be justified. If everyone is marching in a single file, and one person decides to step out of the line, one normally asks that person to explain his change of the status quo. We do not ask those in the line why they were in the line (if there is a fairly obvious reason for a line). As you know, the Jews were in Israel for around 1000 years before Jesus appeared. They had a definite concept of what the Messiah would be like—there was a status quo regarding the nature of the Messiah. The Christians appeared and introduced an entirely different picture of what the Messiah would be like (son of God, God incarnate, born of virgin, two comings, etc.). Thus, the Christians changed the status quo conception of the Messiah, and so the full burden of proof rests upon them. If *they* cannot prove their case thoroughly and conclusively, then *their* thesis must be thrown out. Keep this in mind throughout this book.

The last point that must be clarified before we begin is that this book is a response to Christian missionaries who are trying to convert the Jews. I have nothing against Christian missionaries who try to convert pagans into becoming Christians. That is highly meritorius, because they are then transforming an immoral, primitive person into a more moral and spiritual one. However, that is not true when a Jew becomes a Christian. Therefore, whenever the term "Christian" is used, or if a Christian dogma is criticized, please remember that the real objection is to the Christianity that the Christian missionaries are trying to convert the Jews to. There is a multi-million dollar effort on the part of the Christians to convert as many Jews as they can, and this book is a response to them, not to the rest of the Christians.

SECTION ONE

In this section, all of the basic "proofs" of the divinity of Jesus or "proofs" that he is the real Messiah will be analyzed. There are various pamphlets around which have already done some of this, but none go through all of the basic ones, and the book by Troki[1] would not impress too many potential Christians because of the nature of his answers. In addition, quite often those pamphlets will simply quote the source of the passage, such as Isaiah 53, without quoting any of the verses themselves. The problem with that is that when a person is confronted with the verses and a missionary for the first time, they really can put a person into confusion. This confusion can then be manipulated and taken advantage of—this happens all too often. I personally feel that due to the magnitude of the efforts by the various Christian groups, it would be wise for every person to go through these "proofs" with the various texts in front of him/her, and invite your children and/or friends to join you.

1. Isaac Troki, *Faith Strengthened*, published by Ktav, New York, 1970.

Before we begin, it would be useful to review the basic principles and procedures that were mentioned in the Introduction.

a) Look at the entire context of that verse—start from the beginning of the chapter and continue to the end of it.
b) See if the verse has been translated properly—even Jewish translations are not always precise, so try to find someone who knows Hebrew. Many of their "proofs" rely solely on faulty translation.
c) See if the verse points conclusively and exclusively to Jesus. See if it could just as well apply to someone else, or to a future Messiah who has not yet come. See if an alternative explanation, which would make just as much sense, is possible.

Here are the proofs; the sequence of presentation will be to present the most popular ones first, and the others later.

1. Jeremiah 31:31-34—Here are the relevant quotes: *"Behold, the days come, saith the Lord, that I will make a new covenant with the house of Israel, and with the house of Judah: Not according to the covenant that I made with their fathers in the day that I took them by the hand to bring them out of the land of Egypt, which my covenant they broke. . .But this shall be the covenant that I will make with the house of Israel; after those days, saith the Lord, I will put my law in their inward parts, and write it in their hearts, and will be their God, and they shall be my people. And they shall no more teach every man his neighbor, saying, Know the Lord, for they shall all know me. . .for I will forgive their iniquity, and I will remember their sin no more."*
From this, Christians believe that God told Jeremiah that He would make a new set of laws, a new contract with man. They even call the New Testament the "Bris Chadosha," which is the Hebrew for "a new covenant." This verse is what legitimized the invention of the text and the concepts of the

New Testament, and so we will begin our discussion with this passage.

Here are the problems with this interpretation of the Christians:

a) If the birth of the Christian religion really did introduce the new covenant, then there should no longer be any need for anyone to teach the word of God, *"for they shall know Me."* Since, as everyone with eyes can see, the whole world does not yet recognize God, and the Christians are still trying to teach religion to the world, as are others, it is quite clear that the verse, *"they shall teach no more every man, saying, Know the Lord"* does not apply yet. In other words, the new covenant has *not* taken place yet. It is quite contradictory for the Christians to spend millions of dollars in their attempt to convert the world to Christianity, and to then claim that we live under the terms of the new covenant. However, the Christians claim that they have an answer to this problem. They say that verse 34 *("And they shall teach no more. . .")* refers to the second coming of Jesus. Verse 34 will be fulfilled when Jesus returns once again to visit mankind.

Since we will have to do it sometime, this is an opportune place to thoroughly analyze the doctrine of the second coming. You will discover that whenever any really strong question, such as the one above, is asked, the standard answer is that it refers to the second coming. It therefore becomes extremely important to ascertain the validity of this claim. The success of the Christian claim or its failure rests in a very large way on the theory of the second coming.

First of all, the explanation above that verses 31, 32, and 33 refer to the time of around 29 A.D., and verse 34 applies 2,000 or more years later seems a bit forced, if not absurd. There is no indication whatsoever that that interpretation was intended. It is clearly an answer born of desperation.

In addition, there is a major historical dilemma which seems to explain why the doctrine of the second coming was invented. H.M. Waddams, who was the Residentiary Canon of Canterbury Cathedral in 1968, wrote a book explaining why it took so many years for the Church to get organized into a formal, organized group. His answer is that even though verses such as Matthew 24:34 may mean that Jesus is referring to a future generation (i.e., substitute "that" for "this," which of course is very forced[2]) nonetheless most of the early Christians thought that the simple interpretation was correct. It corroborated the impressions that they had of the message of Jesus, and so they thought that Jesus would return within their own lifetime. After all, Jesus did say, in Matthew 16:28, *"Verily I say unto you, there be some standing here which shall not taste of death, till they see the son of man coming in his kingdom."* However, after many years went by, and the generation that lived in Jesus' generation had all died, it became rather apparent that Jesus would not reappear in the near future. The doctrine was therefore changed so that his reappearance was not necessarily going to be in the near future.[3] (As we will point out later, much of the Christian religion is merely a reaction to beliefs, customs, and unexpected developments that were accepted by or occurred to the people that lived near the early Christians. For example, many Christian holidays are revisions of early pagan holidays.)

Thus, there is an excellent chance that the doctrine of the second coming arose out of a historical dilemma, and not because of the Christian claim that there is a theological dilemma which justified it.

2. Matthew 24 discusses the end of the world, and then, in verse 34, after describing all sorts of unusual prophecies, Jesus says, *"Verily I say unto you, This generation shall not pass, till all these things be fulfilled."* The natural reading of that sentence is that the generation to whom Jesus was talking to would not pass. That is what "this generation" seems to mean—this very generation that I live among. However, the events did not occur during that generation. Later Christians therefore claimed that Jesus meant that when the prophecies began, then the generation that begins to see those events shall not pass away until they are all fulfilled. Thus, the sentence really should read, *"that* generation shall not pass away," which is why the Christian interpretation is forced, and was not really accepted at first.

3. H.M. Waddams, *The Struggle for Christian Unity*, Walker & Co., N.Y., 1968 p. 10.

16

Let us now turn to the supposed theological dilemma. There are verses which indicate that the Messiah will appear in a weak and unglorious fashion, such as Zechariah 9:9, where the Messiah is described coming into Jerusalem *"lowly, and riding on a donkey."* There are, on the other hand, other verses which indicate that he will appear in a mighty, glorious, and ruling fashion, such as Daniel 7:13 and 14, which describe the Messiah coming in on clouds, and *"there was given him dominion, and glory, and kingdom..."* etc. These two verses seem to be the source of the contradiction, and the Christians claim that the Jewish answer is very poor. Let us therefore compare the Jewish with the Christian answer.

The Christians quote two basic Jewish answers, and, in fact, I have not found any more than those two. One answer, mentioned by the Ibn Ezra on Zechariah 9:9, is that Zechariah refers to the Messiah that will be from the house of Joseph (who according to Jewish tradition, will introduce the Messianic Age) and Daniel refers to the Messiah from the house of David. Since the first one will be killed, according to the Talmud, as they explain Zechariah 12:10 (see Talmud Succah 52a), it makes sense to say that both verses of Zechariah refer to the same person. Since his end will be in death, his beginning will be lowly and meek. The other answer is given by the Talmud in Sanhedrin 98a. If the Jews are worthy (i.e., righteous), then the verses of Daniel will apply; if they are not worthy, then the verse of Zechariah 9:9 will apply.

Let us now look at the Christian answer. As you probably have already guessed, Zechariah 9:9 refers to the first coming of Jesus, as does Zechariah 12:10; whereas Daniel 7:13 and 14 refer to the second coming of Jesus.

There are, however, some very major difficulties with their answer. First, if you look at Zechariah 12:10, 11, 12, 13, and 14, it becomes extremely obvious that it does *not* refer to Jesus, because it says that *"I will pour upon the house of David and upon the inhabitants of Jerusalem, the spirit of grace and supplications, and they shall look upon me whom they have pierced* (Christians claim that this refers to Jesus,

17

who was stabbed) *and they shall mourn for him, as one mourns for his only son* (which Christians again points to Jesus, the supposed son of God). *. . .In that day shall there be a great mourning in Jerusalem. . .and the land shall mourn, every family apart. . .all the families that remain. . ."* Now, if this refers to the *first* coming of Jesus, then what was the spirit of grace and supplications—it never seems to have occurred!? In addition, there certainly was no great mourning in Jerusalem and throughout the land by all of the Jewish families after the death of Jesus. On the contrary, since many Jews, according to the Gospels, encouraged the crucifixion, if anything there was a great rejoicing, rather than mourning. Thus, without any doubt, Zechariah 12:10 does not refer to Jesus.

Let us now look at Zechariah 9:9; it is also clearly not referring to Jesus: *"Rejoice greatly, O daughter of Zion. . . behold your King is coming to you, he is just and having salvation; lowly, and riding on a donkey. . .and he shall speak peace unto the heathen, and dominion shall be from sea to sea, and from the river to the ends of the earth. . ."* First of all, Jesus was not the King of the Jews, even if it is true that such a label was placed over his head by the Romans who crucified Jesus. According to Matthew 27:1, all of the chief priests and elders of the people wanted to kill Jesus, and the multitude (27:20) felt the same way about Jesus according to the New Testament. Thus, if Matthew is correct, the Jews did not feel that Jesus was their king. If Matthew is not correct, then the New Testament is false, and the theory of the second coming and the entire Christian religion is also false. In addition, without the Gospels, there is hardly any evidence that Jesus existed in the first place. Even Josephus, who wrote his history very shortly after Jesus was supposed to have been crucified, makes no real mention of Jesus altogether. In his Antiquities of the Jews, Book XVIII, III, 3, there is one small, lonely paragraph about Jesus, and even that does not seem to belong there. That is why many scholars, even Christian, consider this passage in Josephus to be an interpolation by some Christian.[4]

(In the Antiquities, Book XX, IX, 1, Josephus does mention that "the brother of Jesus, who was called Christ, whose name was James" was accused of breaking the law; this is a very meager comment to make regarding a "King" of Israel.[5])

4. Emil Schurer, *A History of the Jewish People in the Time of Jesus*, New York, 1961, page 211. You might also want to read *The Quest for the Historical Jesus* by Albert Schweitzer and the foreword by Wm. LaSor to Whiston's translation of Josephus.

5. See Schurer, for example, page 214, who feels that this passage is also an interpolation by someone other than Josephus. It should be noted that some Christian writers mention an entire list of early historians who seem to affirm the existence of Jesus. However, if you look at them carefully, you will see a general pattern. Tacitus, for example, mentions that a Christus founded a group called Christians, and was put to death by Pontius Pilate—but that's it. There is no mention of any details of how Jesus lived or died, or if this Christus was even called Jesus. None of the early historians describe the life and message of Jesus. Just because they mention that a group called Christians existed hardly verifies all that is written in the Gospels. Some of the Christians' other sources are early Christians, which does not prove anything, because they wrote what they *believed* to be true, not what they saw, for they all lived after the death of Jesus.

It should also be noted that many people erroneously think that the Talmud testifies to the historicity of Jesus, but that is not really true. In the one major passage, Sanhedrin 43b, it mentions that the person called "Yeshu" had five students, whereas the Gospels point out that he had twelve disciples. In a later page in that tractate, page 107b, the same person, Yeshu, is described as the student of Rabbi Yehoshua ben Perachia. Now, if you look in the Talmud, in the Ethics of the Fathers, chapter one, it shows that Rabbi Yehoshua ben Perachia was the teacher of Yehuda ben Tabai and Shimon ben Shetach, who in turn taught Shemaya and Avtalion, who in turn taught Hillel and Shamai. Thus, Rabbi Yehoshua ben Perachia (the teacher of the so called Yeshu) was living around three generations before Hillel, who died around the year 10 A.D. (This is accepted by Jewish historians. For further evidence, the Talmud in Succah 28a states that the smallest—and presumably the youngest—student of Hillel was Rabbi Yochonon ben Zakai. This Rabbi Yochonon ben Zakkai was the same person who spoke with the general who began the siege against Jerusalem, which was completed by Titus—see the Talmud, Gittin 56a, b. Thus, Rabbi Yochonon ben Zakkai lived around 70 A.D., the year Titus destroyed Jerusalem, and he was an old man already, according to the story there, so it makes sense to assume that his teacher was dead for a while). Thus, Jesus, if he is the Yeshu referred to in the Talmud, must have lived around 100 B.C.—which is around three generations before Hillel, but that excludes the person described in the New Testament, who was killed around 30 A.D. at the age of 34, approximately. Thus, there is really no evidence from the Talmud that the Jesus who achieved fame as the founder of Christianity really existed. If anything, the Talmud indicates that the Christian history is incorrect, and that Jesus lived around 100 B.C., and therefore, Jesus never met Pontius Pilate, and therefore, the entire chapter 27 of Matthew is a fabricated lie. Thus, if you accept the Talmud, the Christian story is a lie; if you don't, there is no real evidence for the existence of Jesus altogether.

19

Thus, the New Testament's claim regarding the existence and kingship of Jesus seems to be contradicted by itself as well as other sources.

In addition, Jesus did not *"speak peace to the heathens."* If you look at the end of Acts 10 and the beginning of Acts 11, it is clear that the apostles themselves were shocked that Peter preached to the Gentiles. Now, this makes sense only if they were taught this by Jesus himself—apparently, Jesus made it quite clear that the message was to go to the Jews only. In fact, Paul said this explicitly in Acts 13:46. (See also Matthew 14:24.) So it is clear that Jesus himself never preached to the Gentiles, which therefore excludes Jesus from being the subject of Zechariah 9:10.

Lastly, the subject of the prophecy of Zechariah would have *"dominion from sea to sea, to the ends of the earth."* This, of course was not true then, nor is it true now. The only possible answer the Christians could give is to say that Zechariah 9:9 refers to the first coming, and 9:10 refers to the second, but this is so obviously forced that it need not be discussed. In addition, it makes the entire proof of the second coming fall due to circular reasoning.

It is therefore quite clear that the Christian answer to the apparent contradiction between Zechariah and Daniel cannot be true. I stress this because you will find it difficult to believe that they could have accepted it in the first place. If the Christian answer is clearly untrue, then, consequently, the doctrine of the second coming must similarly be considered to be untrue. It is simply an answer born of desperation due to the inability to answer the strong questions against Christian Biblical interpretations.

Thus, the Christian answer to Jeremiah 31, which is what started this entire discussion, must also be rejected. The new convenant has not occurred yet, and verse 34 does not refer to a "second coming."

In addition, the Christian approach to Jeremiah 31 rests upon one premise, and that premise must be examined. The premise is that a "bris," a covenant, could include a new set of laws. However, if you look throughout the Old Testament, you will find that "bris" does not mean a set of laws, but rather, a creation of a bond, a creation of a closer relationship. Thus, the Christian interpretation, which justifies a new set of laws (Christians do not keep kosher, observe the Sabbath or Yom Kippur, etc.), is built on a false premise in the first place. See Genesis 9:12; God is not commanding the animals; He is creating a relationship with them. See Genesis 15:18; there is no set of laws being commanded or changed. See Deut. 7:2; do not create a close relationship. See Jeremiah himself, in 22:9—because they broke their close relationship with God and worshipped other gods instead. If it meant, because they broke the laws, then why specify that they also worshipped other gods? It would be as if one would say that not only did you murder, but you also robbed! Look us these verses and you will see that a "bris"—a covenant, never refers to a set of laws, and so the missionaries are really using this verse by mistake.

Before we move on to another "proof," there is another important point to be made. It seems clear from the entire Torah that something essential is missing, because if you carefully examine it, it is not very precise at all. For example, look at the Ten Commandments in Exodus, chapter 20. It says that one should not do any work on the Sabbath—but it does not define work, and nowhere in the Torah does it explicitly define what constitutes "work." How then does one know how to obey this law? It says *"honor your father and mother"*—but how does one do that? Must a person obey his parents' wishes that he marry someone who he hates but his parents like? Must he or she reject a job that his or her parents dislike but he or she desires it? Must a child stand up every time a parent walks into the room? You see, there is no real guideline here. If you say, use common sense, that does not help. Many people have a different feeling for what is "common" sense, and therefore you cannot really know if your conclusion is, in fact, the will of God. It does not make sense to claim that God commanded such vague and obscure guidelines. Even the next few laws are unclear. *"Thou shall not murder"*—how do you define murder? If the state allows a type of killing, such as ancient Greece allowing defective children to be left to die on a mountain, is that no longer murder? Is it murder to kill an unborn child, or is it murder only if the child is born? This analysis can be done with virtually every law in the Torah, and so one is faced with the following choice: either God commanded obscure guidelines (and that does not seem quite Godlilike, since even we mortals are sure to give very precise commands to our own children), or else He defined each law, but did not put it down on paper. Jewish tradition says that the second choice is, in fact, what happened. God defined each law, and taught his definition to Moses, who in turn taught the rest of the Jews. This oral definition of the Torah (written law) became known as the Oral Law. In Deuteronomy 17:8-13, the Jews were also commanded that if a doubt would arise in any area of Jewish Law, they should go to the Sanhedrin, the high court, and what they interpret the law to be, will become, in fact, the will of God. (That is how the Oral Law understands those verses.)

This is actually, historically, how the Jews functioned in classical times. Even the New Testament agrees that that is how the Jewish society was run; i.e., under the Sanhedrin. So now we have a basic question which is extremely basic and crucial. If, as history and the New Testament agree, the vast majority of Jews, and the Sanhedrin, rejected Jesus as the real Messiah, and the Sanhedrin thought that Jesus did not fit the qualifications for being a bona-fide Messiah, according to their interpretations of the Bible, then we should follow the opinion of the Sanhedrin. This is merely a matter of interpreting Jeremiah 31 or Isaiah 53, etc., and when it comes to Biblical interpretation, we are commanded by God to follow the Sanhedrin.

Both the Sanhedrin as well as the majority of Jews who lived *at the time of Jesus* rejected him, according to Paul in Acts 13:46, and they rejected the Christian interpretations of the Bible. How, then, is any Jew permitted to accept Christian interpretation today? Could a person also accept Christian interepretations of how to honor one's parents? Would it also be permitted to accept the Christian interpretation of "do not murder?" (Always remember that the Church initiated the Crusades, during which thousands of Jews were killed in the name of Jesus. In addition, remember that the Church was against the shedding of blood because of the command, *"Thou shalt not murder."* Therefore, during the Inquisition, they killed thousands of Jews who had been forced to convert by *burning* them, sometimes *alive*, so that no blood would be spilled! The Christian interpretation was that it was wrong to spill or shed blood, but if you strangle someone or burn him, that would be permitted, and that is one of the reasons why they burned people at the stake.[6])

Thus, that is the choice—who is to interpret the Bible, and that is the question—why did almost all of the Jews reject Jesus as the Messiah, and in addition, the Christian interpretations of the Bible? (Part of the reason must be because the interpretations are forced, if not terrible, but you could decide that for yourself, so keep on reading. We will go through many more of their interpretations.) The Jews never had a notion of a second coming, and since it was the Jews themselves who taught the notion of a Messiah in the first place, via Jewish prophets, it seems quite reasonable to respect their opinion more than anyone else's. As we pointed out in the Introduction, it was the Christians who were changing the status quo, and so they ought to have very substantial reasons for doing so. As you will see, their reasons and proofs are not substantial at all, and they therefore have yet to justify their change of the status quo.

2. Isaiah 53—Here are the relevant quotes (starting from Isaiah 52:13): *"Behold my servant shall deal prudently, he shall be exalted and extolled, and be very high. As many were astonished at thee; his visage was so marred more than any man, and his form more than the sons of men. So shall he*

6. Cecil Roth, *A History of the Marranos*, Meridian, 1960, page 124.

sprinkle many nations; the kings shall shut their mouths at him, for that which had not been told them shall they see, and that which they had not heard shall they consider. Who hath believed our report? and to whom is the arm of the Lord revealed? For he shall grow up before him as a tender plant, and as a root out of dry ground: he hath no form nor comeliness: and when we shall see him, there is no beauty that we should desire him. He is despised and rejected of men; a man of sorrows, and acquainted with grief: and we hid as it were our faces from him: he was despised, and we esteemed him not. Surely he hath born our griefs, and carried our sorrows, yet we did esteem him stricken, smitten of God, and afflicted. But he was wounded for our transgressions, he was bruised for our iniquities. . .and with his stripes we are healed. . .the Lord hath laid on him the iniquity of us all. . .he was oppressed and he was afflicted, yet he opened not his mouth; he is brought as a lamb to the slaughter. . .and he made his grave with the wicked. . .

This passage is one of the most quoted passages. It is used to prove that the person referred to in Isaiah 53 is the same person (Jesus) that is referred to in Matthew 26 and 27, which describes the plotting of the Jews to kill Jesus (thus, he was despised), the binding of Jesus and the delivering of Jesus to the Romans, after which Jesus made no answer to the accusations presented (brought as a lamb, yet he opened not his mouth); he was on trial at the same time as a murderer (Luke 23:25), and was crucified with two robbers (and made his grave with the wicked).

There are many problems with this "proof." Here are some of them:

a) Does the text point exclusively to Jesus? The answer is clearly—no. Many Jewish commentators feel that it refers to the Jewish people on the whole. We find many instances in the Bible where the Jewish people on the whole are addressed to, or are described, in the singular, such as the very famous, *"Hear, O Israel, the Lord who is our God, is one"* (Deuteronomy 6:4); the verb "hear" there is singular in the Hebrew original. See also, in the Hebrew, Deuteronomy 4:10 ("omadtah"). The Ten Commandments in Exodus 20 are in the singular, in the Hebrew, and yet were addressed to the entire people. Exodus 18:13—*"the nation stood"*—in the singular, again. Exodus 19:2—*"camped,"* in the singular, again. There are many such instances like this in Isaiah as well, if you look in the original Hebrew.[7] Thus, while you will find many places where the plural is used, you will also find many places where the singular is used to describe the entire people. Thus, Isaiah 53 could very well be describing the history of the Jewish people—despised by the world, persecuted by the Crusaders and the Spanish Inquisition and the Nazis, while the world silently watched. (You might want to read *The History of Anti-Semitism* by Leon Poliakov for an excellent description of Christian anti-Semitism, as well as *The Anguish of the Jews*, by Edward Flannery, a Catholic priest, in addition to *While Six Million Died* by Arthur Morse.) The nation of Israel suffers in silence; they are accused of being evil by those who are truly evil. Isaiah himself, *only four chapters earlier*, calls the Jewish people the *same term* that he used here—*"my servant"* (Isaiah 49:3). There it *again is in the singular*, and it explicitly says there that it refers to the Jewish people. Thus, in Isaiah 49:6, Isaiah says that the Jews are to be a light to all of the nations, and are therefore more responsible, and therefore Isaiah points out in chapter 53 that the Jews will bear the iniquity of the world. This is a very simple, unforced, smooth understanding of the verses.

The verses therefore do not point exclusively to Jesus, or to a Messiah, and so this passage is no proof whatsoever to Christianity.

b) If you look at the passage closely, you will discover an amazing difficulty with the Christian interpretation—the verbs keep changing tenses. Isaiah 53:2 says that *"he shall grow up as a tender plant"*—this is referring to the future (shall grow). The next verse says, *"He is despised and rejected"*—this

7. See Isaiah 1:3; 40:27; 41:8.

refers to the present, presumably the time of Isaiah himself. The next verse says, *"surely he has born our griefs and carried out sorrows"*—this in the past tense. The next verse reads, *"But he was wounded for our transgressions. . ."*— again past tense. Now, if this passage refers to Jesus, then something is very difficult, for if Isaiah is speaking about the future growth of a plant, and if that refers to Jesus, then how could the following verses, which refer to the past, refer to Jesus? If you say that the entire passage refers to the future, then why did Isaiah change tenses? The Jewish explanation above has none of these difficulties. Isaiah is saying that the Jewish people will develop into a plant, a source of nourishment for the world, but at the time Isaiah is speaking, the world despises the Jew, and the Jew has already been afflicted by the Egyptians,[8] the Philistines,[9] etc., and all of the affliction has been an atonement for the sins of the Jewish people. This explanation fits very nicely, unlike the Christian one.

c) Try using the Jews in Auschwitz as the subject of Isaiah 53; it works out just as well, if not better, than Jesus. Perhaps Isaiah is referring to them? Thus, again, the passage does not point exclusively to Jesus.

d) Perhaps Isaiah 53 refers to the Messiah, and perhaps the Messiah will be despised, etc.—but perhaps this Messiah has not come yet? So what if Jesus suffered, perhaps the real Messiah will also suffer, and so perhaps Isaiah 53 refers to the future Messiah. There is no *proof* that it refers to Jesus even if the passage refers to a Messiah.

e) This comment is important to this passage, but, in addition, to the entire New Testament on the whole. The entire "proof" rests on one premise, and that is that the history of the life of Jesus is portrayed honestly and correctly by the New Testament. This, however, can be greately questioned, for the following reason. If you read Matthew chapter 27, you will see Pontius Pilate described as *peace loving, justice seeking,*

8. See Exodus, chapter one.
9. See Judges 13:1; 1 Samuel 14:52.

decent fellow. Pilate keeps asking, *"Why, what evil has he (Jesus) done?"* See Luke 23:22—*"And he* (Pontius) *said unto them* (the Jews) *the third time, why, what evil has he done?"* And so, in Matthew 27:24, Pontius washes his hands to indicate his complete innocence of the death of Jesus. Pontius, according to the Gospels, was pressured by the clamoring Jews to crucify Jesus, and so he had to give in. So it seems that Pontius is a weak ruler who wants to be just and moral. This is the picture of the New Testament.

However, historians seem to disagree. Emil Schurer, in his history of the period, quotes Philo's description of Pontius as "an unbending and recklessly hard character; corruptibility, violence, robberies, ill treatment of the people, grievances, continuous executions without even the form of a trial, endless and intolerable cruelties" are charged against him.[10] Josephus, in his Wars of the Jews, Book II, Chapter IX, shows how Pontius began his career with the Jews with a major change, which almost caused enormous bloodshed, and then continued to cause disturbances, during which many Jews were killed. In his Antiquities, Book XVIII, IV, 1, 2, Josephus shows that his excessive murders eventually got Pontius recalled to Rome! And so, if you look in various histories of the period, you will see Pontius Pilate portrayed in exactly the *opposite* manner as he is portrayed in the New Testament. This forces one to say that the authors of the Gospels doctored the story so that Jesus comes out looking innocent, Pontius comes out looking innocent, and the Jews looking guilty. Once you find one place where the authors lied, or twisted the facts, you could assume it could happen elsewhere. Thus, Isaiah 53 seems to resemble the crucifixion, but only if the history of the Jesus story is honest and correct. That, however, is very questionable. Read *The Passover Plot* by Schonfield; keep in mind that if you were making up a story about someone whom you thought was the Messiah, you would also try to doctor the story so that it resembled the description written hundreds of

10. See ibid, page 198.

years before, in the book of Isaiah, about the Messiah (if, indeed, it is talking about the Messiah in the first place). (See page 72, question A5, for more questions along these lines.)

f) There is another problem, and this too is based on the text itself. Isaiah says that the person referred to *"is brought as a lamb to the slaughter; and as a sheep before her shearers is dumb, so he openeth not his mouth"* (verse 7). Now, whoever this verse is referring to, one thing is certain—it certainly is not referring to Jesus. If you look in Matthew 27:46, you will see that Jesus, while he was crucified, not only was not silent, but he even seems to be blaspheming, for he cried out *"with a loud voice, "My God, my God, why hast Thou forsaken me?"* Jesus is crying out to God, and he accuses God of forsaking him.

That certainly is not the silent sheep of Isaiah 53, who was not to cry out in a loud voice, nor was he to blaspheme and accuse God in public. Perhaps Isaiah 53 refers to those Jewish martyrs who were killed by the Roman Hadrian one hundred years later, and who died with love of God on their hearts. The Talmud (Berochos 61b) relates that when Rabbi Akiva was being killed during that period, he died with the Shma on his lips, even while the Romans were raking the skin off his body with an iron rake. Rabbi Akiva died a more painful death than Jesus, or at least as painful, and yet Rabbi Akiva died with the love of God on his mouth. He did not accuse God of forsaking him. Thus, Isaiah 53 applies more to Rabbi Akiva than to Jesus. No matter what, Isaiah 53 cannot refer to Jesus, because Jesus did not go silently as a lamb to his death.

g) In Isaiah 53:10, it says that *"he shall see his seed, he shall prolong his days."* This means that the subject of Isaiah 53 will have children and live a long life. Since neither of these was true in the life of Jesus, Isaiah 53 cannot refer to Jesus. It could, however, refer quite easily to the Jewish people.

3. Daniel 9:24-27—Here are the quotes from the New Testament: *"Seventy weeks are determined upon thy people and upon the holy city, to finish the transgression, and to make an end of sins, and to make reconciliation of iniquity,* *and to bring in everlasting righteousness, and to seal up the vision and prophecy, and to anoint the most Holy. Know therefore and understand, that from the going forth of the commandment to restore and to build Jerusalem unto the Messiah the Prince shall be seven weeks, and sixty two weeks; the street shall be built again, and the wall, even in troubled times. And after sixty two weeks shall the Messiah be cut off, but not for himself, and the people of the prince that shall come shall destroy the city and the sanctuary; and the end thereof shall be with a flood, and unto the end of the war desolations are determined. And he shall confirm the covenant with many for one week, and in the midst of the week he shall cause the sacrifice and oblation to cease, and for the overspreading of abominations he shall make it desolate, even unto the consumation, and that determined shall be poured upon the desolate."*

This passage is one of their favorites, and by using a few mistranslations and misplaced commas, they end up with an amazing, though very clever, interpretation.

Here is the Christian interpretation:

The Artaxerxes of Nehemiah 2:1 rose to power in 465 B.C., and so, according to Nehemiah 2:1, the commandment to restore Jerusalem began 20 years later, i.e., 445 B.C. Now, since they claim that a Biblical year had 360 days, they multiply 360 by 483 (69 weeks equals 69 periods of seven years—69 X 7 = 483 years). This equals 173,880 days. To change from Biblical years to our solar years, they divide 173,880 days by 365¼; this equals 476 years. Add 476 years to 445 B.C. and you will get 31 A.D. Actually, they add a few days, and it ends up around 32 A.D., which is just when they claim that Jesus was crucified. Thus, Daniel 9:25, when discussing the Messiah, is referring to Jesus, saying that he will be *"cut off"* i.e., crucified.

There are really many difficulties with this interpretation, which is why the Jews were never impressed with it.

The first problem is that they mistranslated the main verse, verse 25. The way they read it is that after seven weeks and sixty two weeks, the Messiah will come; i.e., after 69 weeks, the Messiah will come. The obvious question is—why didn't Daniel simply write 69 weeks, instead of writing 7 plus 62? The answer is that they mistranslated the verse. If you translate it correctly, that question disappears. Here is the correct translation: Know and discern that from the going forth of the word to restore and build Jerusalem unto one anointed, a prince, shall be seven weeks; and for sixty two weeks shall it be built again with streets and moats, but in troublesome times. Note the main difference—not that it will take 69 weeks before the Messiah will come, but rather a mere 7 weeks. If you study this in the original Hebrew, this should be quite clear. Thus, the translation by itself answers the above question of why not simply write 69, instead of 7 plus 62. According to the correct translation, the anointed one will come after 7 weeks, the city will remain built for 62 weeks, and after the 62 weeks, (verse 26) it will be destroyed. The Christian translation cannot explain why Daniel had to mention the first seven weeks, and in fact it is a mistranslation. Thus, if they show you their Bible, open the original and show them the difference.

Another major difficulty is that according to the simple, untwisted translation of verse 26, two events were to occur after the 62 weeks—the anointed one would be cut off, *and* the city and the sanctuary would be destroyed. As you know, Jerusalem was destroyed in 70 A.D., which is 38 years after the death of Jesus—more than five "weeks" off. There is no *decent* answer for this missing five weeks according to the Christian interpretation.

Another difficulty is that the Jewish year is not really 360 days long. While the months are based on the lunar patterns, the years must coincide with the solar system. See Maimonides, Laws of Kiddush HaChodesh 1:1, 2 for this, or simply study the Jewish calendar. You will see that since the solar year exceeds the lunar year by around 11 days, there will be an extra month added around every three years. Thus 445 B.C. plus 483 years (69 X 7) ends up 38 A.D., and by then everybody admits that Jesus was dead already.

Another difficulty is that the Christians, for lack of a better answer, claim that the 70th week will take place when Jesus returns in his second coming as a king. The problem was caused because Daniel mentioned a total of 70 weeks, and then he specified 7 plus 62, leaving one remaining. The Christians say that the first 69 weeks were consecutive, then there is at least a *1900 year gap*, and sooner or later the 70th week will occur. This is obviously a very forced explanation, born of desperation.

There is one other point that should be made. If you examine the other books of the Bible, it becomes quite apparent that Daniel is referring to Cyrus, of Persia, and not Jesus. In Jermiah 25:11, 12, the word of God clearly states that the Babylonian exile will last for only 70 years. In Ezra 1:1, it says that *"Now in the first year of Cyrus, king of Persia, that the word of the Lord by the mouth of Jeremiah might be fulfilled, the Lord stirred up the spirit of Cyrus, king of Persia, that he made a proclamation throughout all his kingdom. . .saying . . .Whosoever there is among you of all His people, let him go to Jerusalem, and build the house of the Lord. . ."* In Isaiah 45:1, it says, *"Thus saith the Lord to his anointed, to Cyrus. . ."* Thus, Isaiah, in the name of God, calls Cyrus an anointed one, and Ezra discusses how Cyrus fulfilled the prophecy of Jeremiah. Since Daniel lived after Isaiah and Jeremiah but before the period of Ezra,[11] it is most reasonable and probable to affirm that the anointed one that he referred to in Daniel 9:25 is Cyrus, and not Jesus.

The reason why a Christian would have difficulty understanding this is because the compiler of the King James Bible was a shrewd person. In the original Hebrew, both Daniel 9:25 and Isaiah 45:1 use the exact same word—"moshiach." However, in the New Testament, the word, "moshiach," is translated in Isaiah 45:1 as "anointed" whereas in Daniel

---

11. See Daniel 1:1-6. Daniel was a child, or young lad, at the beginning of the Babylonian Exile. Ezra became prominent after the Babylonian Exile was over—see Ezra 7:1.

9:25, the same Hebrew word is translated as "the Messiah." ("Messiah" is the Anglicized version of "Moshiach"; the pure translation of "Moshiach" is "an anointed one.") This deceptive translating makes it virtually impossible for the innocent reader who does not know Hebrew to discern the truth. In addition, the compiler of the New Testament did one other clever maneuver. The sequence of the various books of the Bible are arranged in the New Testament in a rather peculiar manner: the Pentateuch, Samuel, Chronicles, then Ezra, and then Esther, Job, Psalms, Proverbs, Ecclesiastes, Song of Songs, Isaiah, Jeremiah, Lamentations, Ezekiel, and then Daniel. (In the Jewish Bible, Ezra follows all of the above.) The reason for placing Ezra in the New Testament before Isaiah, and before Psalms, Proverbs, etc., even though Ezra lived long after those books were written is presumably to fool the reader of the New Testament. Had the reader read Ezra immediately after Daniel, which is the correct chronological location, the reader would immediately recognize that Ezra 1:1 and Daniel 9:25 refer to Cyrus, and not Jesus.

4. Psalm 22—The Christians claim that this chapter refers to Jesus, so let us look at the relevant quotes: *"My God, my God, why have you forsaken me, why are you so far from helping me, and from the words of my roaring? O my God, I cry in the daytime, but Thou hearest not. . .Our fathers trusted in You; they trusted and were delivered. . .But I am a worm, and no man; a reproach of men, and despised of the people. All they that see me laugh me to scorn, they shoot out the lip, they shake the head, saying, He trusted on the Lord that He would deliver him; let Him deliver him, seeing he delighted in Him. . .I was cast upon Thee from the womb; Thou art my God from my mother's belly. Be not far from me; for trouble is near, there is none to help. Many bulls have compassed me. . .they gaped upon me with their mouths as a ravening and a roaring lion. I am poured out like water, and all my bones are out of joint; my heart is like wax; it is melted in the midst of my bowels. My strength is dried up like a* potsherd, and my tongue cleaveth to my jaws, and Thou hast brought me into the dust of death. For dogs have compassed me; the assembly of the wicked have enclosed me; they pierced my hands and my feet. . . They part my garments among them, and cast lots upon my vesture. But be not Thou far from me, O Lord, O my strength, haste to help me. Deliver my soul from the sword. . .save me from the lion's mouth. . ."

From this Christians claim that it refers to Jesus, who was also rejected by his own people, and who was taunted and mocked; see Matthew 26 and 27 for a description of that. This passage also, supposedly, refers to the crucifixion of Jesus ("my bones are out of joint. . .they pierced my hands and feet. . .").

This passage has its difficulties as well. The critical question is— does Psalm 22 point exclusively and necessarily to Jesus, or can it refer to others as well? The answer is clear—it could refer to someone besides Jesus. Many commentators felt that it refers to the Jewish people on the whole; the singular is often used in that siutation (see earlier page 24). Kind David, the author of this Psalm, may be asking God why would the Jewish people be occasionally forsaken throughout history, especially when the Jews were suffering under the Nazis. The Jews were a despised people, especially when no country wanted to allow them to immigrate, in the late 1930's, or under the British Mandate. Many bulls surrounded the Jews, from the Crusaders to the Cossacks to the Nazis. The assembly of the wicked have enclosed the Jews, and parted their garments, such as when the Nazis separated all of their garments and even the fillings from their mouths. Thus, Psalm 22 does not necessarily point to Jesus at all. In fact, verse 17—"I may tell all my bones" implies that the person may be starving and the ribs are showing, which was not true of Jesus, but was true of the Jews in Auschwitz. Furthermore, Jesus did not expect God to deliver him—there is no indication anywhere that Jesus expected to be rescued. On the contrary, he expected to be crucified (Matthew 20:19). This contradicts verse 8, which states that the subject of this Psalm expected to be rescued

TEMPLE ISRAEL LIBRARY

(*"He trusted on the Lord that He would deliver him. . ."*).
Furthermore, the only reason we would think that this Psalm
refers to Jesus is because the history described in the New
Testament seems to indicate a similarity between the crucifixion story and this Psalm. But the problem remains, how do
we know if the history of the New Testament is true, or was it
doctored to make Jesus look like the subject of Psalm 22 (see
earlier pages 26, 27). Since the story about Pontius Pilate
seems to have been doctored, one must suspect every part of
the story and accept the possibility that other parts were
doctored as well.

One other point must be pointed out, in addition, and this is
that the New Testament mistranslated a verse to its obvious
benefit. That verse of *"they pierced my hands and my feet,"*
which seems to point to Jesus, is a mistranslation, according to
all of the classical Jewish scholars, who knew Hebrew perfectly. In fact, the Christians have invented a new word in the
process, which is still not in the Hebrew dictionary, for to them
the Hebrew word, "Koari" means "pierced." There is no such
Hebrew word—look in a modern or ancient Hebrew dictionary. The real translation is, "like a lion." In other words, here
is the verse: *"For dogs have surrounded me, the assembly of
the wicked have enclosed me, like a lion (who has) my hands
and my feet."*

5. Micah 5:1, 2—Here are the quotes: (in the Old Testament, it is 4:13; 5:1) *"Now gather thyself in troops, O
daughter of troops; he has laid seige against us: they shall
smite the judge of Israel with a rod upon the cheek. But thou,
Bethlehem Ephratah, though thou be little among the thousands of Judah, yet out of thee shall he come forth unto me
that is going to be ruler in Israel; whose goings forth have been
from of old, from everlasting."*

From this the Christians have deduced that Jesus was to be
smitten and attacked by his enemies (*"they shall smite the
judge of Israel"*); that Jesus was to be born in Bethlehem (*But
as for you, Bethelehem. . .from you shall go forth. . ."*); and
that Jesus existed even before he was born in his physical form.

The flaws in those deductions should be self evident. The last deduction is simply a figment of someone's imagination, since the verse is not discussing pre-existence preceding corporality. But the real issue is: is this verse talking about Jesus in the first place? And the answer again is—not at all. The verse seems to refer explicitly to David, since it parallels 1 Samuel 17:12—*"Now David was the son of that Ephrathite of Bethlehem..."* The verse is saying, You, David, thought you ought to be (see the original Hebrew; the New Testament mistranslated this verse as well) little among the thousands of Judah (according to the commentaries—because he came from Ruth, the Moabite), yet from you will come the Messiah. It does not say that the Messiah will be born in Bethlehem, but that the father (the distant father) will be born in Bethlehem.[12] In addition, this Messiah mentioned here is to bring peace (verse 5) which Jesus most certainly did not do, as evidenced by the world wars and nuclear warheads that have become part of normal modern life. Furthermore, since many thousands of children were born in Bethlehem, even if the verse were discussing the birthplace of the Messiah, it would not prove anything. Just because Jesus may have been born there, in itself, does not distinguish him from the other thousands of children who were born there.

As far as the first verse, regarding the smiting of Jesus, it simply and only says *"the judge of Israel."* Whoever he may be, it probably was not Jesus, since he was not a judge. In fact, he told his few followers, in Matthew 7:1, *"Judge not, so that ye be not judged."* To say that the subject of Micah 5:1 is Jesus is to call Jesus a hypocrite.

Last, but not least, there is a basic question altogether as to whether or not Jesus came from David in the first place. In Matthew chapter 1, ther is an entire geneology which purports

12. The line, "whose goings forth has been from old, from everlasting" (or, as the Hebrew has it, "from the days of the world"), would mean that the concept of the Messiah, the concept of the Messianic actualization of peace and fulfillment, is from the time of creation itself. This thought can be found in the Midrash in Breishis Rabba, 2:4.

to show that Jesus does indeed come from David. However, there is a very serious problem there, for the geneology shows that Joseph, the husband of Mary (who was the Mother of Jesus) was from David, but he was *not* the father of Jesus. What is the point of showing that Joseph is from David, if Joseph is not the father of Jesus? In fact, in verse 19, Joseph, *"being a righteous man, and not wanting to disgrace her, desired to put her away privately."* He obviously thought that Mary committed adultery and that the son was illegitimate. Thus, according to the New Testament itself, Jesus was not from Joseph. In fact, the geneology of the New Testament proves that Jesus was *not* from David. Jesus is considered by the New Testament to be a child of God, who is *not* from the tribe of Judah, nor any other tride. Jesus is therefore not the subject of Micah 5:1 or 2. (See page 78, question B2, for an elaboration of this point.)

6. Deuteronomy 18:15, 18—Here are the quotes: *"The Lord thy God will raise up unto thee a Prophet from the midst of thee, of thy brethren, like unto me; unto him you shall hearken. . .I will raise up a Prophet from among their brethren, like unto thee, and will put My words in his mouth. . ."*

From this the Christians have deduced that Jesus is a prophet of God, and that whatever he said was the word of God. This, of course, is absolutely amazing. The verse simply said that there will be other people like Moses; namely, there will be prophets, or, there will another prophet. Who this prophet is was not specified, but the Christians themselves recognize Jeremiah, Isaiah, Micah, and the others in the Torah as prophets, so this verse refers at least to them. In fact, the New Testament itself, while commenting on *this* verse of Deuteronomy, explicitly calls Samuel a prophet (see Acts 3:22-24). Thus, we are simply told that other people will arise who will be similar to Moses—that there will be another man who will communicate with God, and relay the message back to man. The only question left is—was Jesus included in this verse along with the other prophets? The people of Israel who lived in Israel at the time of Jesus thought that Jesus was the subject of the *next* passage of Deuteronomy, *not this one.* The next passage, in Deut. 18:20, says, *"But the prophet which shall presume to speak a word in My name, which I have not commanded him to speak. . .even that prophet shall die."* Since, as it is well known, the Christians do not obey the laws of the Torah—they do not keep kosher, or observe the Shabbat, for example—and they attribute this change to the coming of Jesus, the Jewish people have always felt that verse 20 applies to Jesus, not verse 18. Of course, the Christians feel that Jeremiah 31 legitimized the abrogation of the Mosaic law, but we have already demonstrated the error of that argument. Thus, there is no proof that verses 15 and 18 refers to Jesus, whereas there is reason to assume that verse 20 does apply to him.

7. **Psalm 110**—Here are the relevant quotes: *"The Lord said unto my Lord, sit at my right hand, until I make your enemies your footstool. The Lord shall send the rod of your strength out of Zion; rule in the midst of your enemies. The people shall be willing in the day of your power, in the beauties of holiness from the womb of the morning; you have the dew of your youth. The Lord has sworn, and will not repent. You are a priest forever after the order of Melchizedek . . ."*

From this passage the Christians have proved that Jesus sits at God's right side, and that Jesus should be called Lord, and that he is a Lord or God (*"The Lord said unto my* Lord"*).

Once again, this interpretation rests on a mistranslation. In the original Hebrew, it reads that God said "l'adonee"—i.e., "to my master." In addition, the passage begins with the words, "A Psalm to David" which the King James Bible has in very tiny print, separated from the main passage, which the Hebrew original does not do. Thus, the passage begins: a Psalm to David—God said to my master. . .(note that in the original Hebrew as well as in the King James Bible, it reads, "said" in the past tense.). Now, who is David's master? Could it be someone who was not born yet, such as Jesus? That seems very absurd and forced. Therefore, the Talmud says it refers to Abraham, our forefather, and the Psalm refers to the anxious time before Abraham had to fight the four kings, in Genesis 14. God is telling Abraham not to worry, sit, so to speak, at my side, until I take care of your enemies. A proof of this explanation seems to be from the reference to Malchizedek, who is mentioned in *only* one other place in the Bible, and that is *also* in Genesis 14 (verse 18), and it describes him there in terms of a priest also. So it is clear that the verse does not point exclusively to Jesus at all, and more so, it does seem to point directly to someone else, namely, Abraham, who was a master, in some way, to David, and who had a relationship to Malchizedek.

8. Zechariah 12:10—This is the verse about someone being pierced, and mourned for as on only child. The Christians like this proof, but it is full of difficulties, which were already pointed out earlier on pages 17 and 18.

9. Isaiah 7:14—Here are the relevant quotes, starting from the beginning of the chapter: *"And it came to pass in the days of Ahaz, the son of Jotham, the son of Uzziah, king of Judah, that Rezin, king of Syria, and Pekah the son of Remaliah, king of Israel, went up towards Jerusalem to war against it. And it was told the house of David, saying, Syria is confederate with Ephraim. And his heart was moved, and the heart of his people. . .Then said the Lord unto Isaiah, go forth now to meet Ahaz. . .say unto him, take heed and be quiet; fear not, neither be fainthearted for the two tails of these smoking firebrands, for the fierce anger of Rezin with Syria, and of the son of Remaliah. . .Thus saith the Lord God, it shall not stand, neither shall it come to pass. . .Moreover, the Lord spoke again unto Ahaz, saying, Ask a sign of the Lord thy God. . .But Ahaz said, I will not ask, neither will I tempt the Lord. And he said, Hear now, O house of David, Is it a small thing for you to weary men, but will you weary my God also.*

(verse 14) Therefore the Lord Himself shall give you a sign; Behold a virgin shall conceive, and bear a son, and shall call his name Immanuel. . ."
This verse (7:14) is the source behind the virgin birth theory, indicating that the Messiah will be born of a virgin, and that the Messiah is Jesus, who was also supposedly born from a virgin.

However, if one reads the entire chapter, one sees the flaw immediately. The birth of the child, Immanuel, was to be a sign from God to King Ahaz, who lived at least 500 years before Jesus. If the Christians are correct, then God is an idiot, for He is promising a sign to Ahaz that will convince Ahaz not to worry at all about the two invading armies, and this sign will appear 500 years later! This is obviously absurd. In addition, as many modern scholars now admit, the word that caused the whole "proof" was mistranslated: "almah" does not mean virgin in Biblical Hebrew; "b'sullah" is the word used for that. Ask any Hebrew scholar to corroborate that, or check many of the new Christian Bibles, such as the Revised Standard Version. In addition, Jesus was never called Immanuel. See Matthew 1:21-23—*"thou shalt call his name Jesus, that it might be fulfilled which was spoken by the prophet, saying, Behond a virgin shall be with child, and shall bring forth a son, and they shall call his name Immanuel."* How does that make sense—they were to call his name Immanuel, and instead they called him Jesus!

Lastly, it is important to recognize the origin of the theory of the virgin birth. The Jews never had such a theory, so why did the Christians invent it? The answer is clear: the Jews rejected Jesus, and the Gentiles were about to do the same (see Acts 15). So Paul did two things—he issued an order saying that to be a Christian one no longer had to obey the 613 commandments of the Torah that the Jews had to observe (see Acts 15), and in addition, Paul introduced a few pagan myths into the new Christian relition so that it would appeal to the pagan Gentiles.

Thus, if you look in that famous book of pagan rituals, *The Golden Bough*, by Frazer, chapter 34 (in the abridged edition), there is a discussion about the god called Attis, which was worshipped in Western Asia (which, if I may remind you, is not too far from the Middle East, where Paul lived and preached). Attis, Frazer points out, was born from a virgin. Attis was killed afterwards; one theory is that he was killed by a boar; the other theory is that he cut off his genitals under a tree and bled to death. Thus, in the annual holiday commemorating the death of Attis, *in Syria*, man after man would leap forth with a shout, grab a handy sword, and would castrate himself on the spot. Then, read carefully, an effigy of Attis was hung, and afterwards was buried in a sepulchre. Then the tomb would be opened, the god Attis would rise from the dead, and he would softly whisper glad tidings of salvation. The next day, which would be the vernal equinox, on the twenty-fifth of March, the divine resurrection would be celebrated with great joy. At Rome, the celebration took the form of a carnival. In addition, there was a sacramental meal and a baptism (that is the word Frazer uses) of blood, where a person went into a pit, had a bull's blood poured on him, covering him completely, and then was considered by his fellow as one who had been born again to eternal life and had washed away his sins in the blood of the bull.

The roots of Christianity are an exact pattern of the above worship of Attis: the virgin birth of Attis and Jesus, the celibacy promoted by Paul in 1 Corinthians 7:8, 9 *("I say therefore to the unmarried and widows, it is good for them if they abide as I; but if they cannot contain, let them marry, for it is better to marry than to burn."* The celibacy is the Christian form of castration.), Jesus was crucified just as Attis was hung, and Jesus was placed in a sepulchre, just as Attis was. The tomb of both of them were opened, a resurrection was supposed to have taken place in both instances, with a message of good tidings and salvation occurring again in both situations. All this was to occur, in both instances, around the beginning of Spring. Lastly, this identical worship of Attis and Jesus took place in the same locations—Syria, Rome, etc.[13]

The Christian religion is so identical with the worship of Attis that it cannot be considered a coincidence. Rather, Paul introduced the pagan ideas of his neighborhood into the worship of Jesus, and made a new religion which would be perfectly compatible with the Gentile pagans in the neighborhood. Paul simply switched Jesus for Attis, put a little Judaism in, and then called it Christianity.

Thus, the concern about the virgin birth does not stem from a search for the true interpretation of Isaiah, but because it fit in to the pagan myths. Study the pagan myths, see the similarities to Christianity, and then you will begin to really understand Christianity. You will discover that many of the Christian holidays are based on pagan holidays, and that many of the rituals are based on pagan origins. See 1 Corinthians 10:16-21; Paul is saying that the drinking of wine, which symbolizes the drinking of the blood of Jesus, should not be confused with the pagan cups drunk by the pagans. Study the history of the origin of the holiday of Christmas; you will discover that the pagans always had a major holiday around December 25, rejoicing the end of the winter solstice. Sunday, the day of the week dedicated to the pagan god—the Sun, which they worshipped—became the day of the week that was designated as special, instead of the original day of Saturday, which Jesus used as the day of rest.[14]

10. Isaiah 64:6—Here are the quotes: *"But we are all as an unclean thing, and all our righteousnesses are as filthy rags; and we all do fade as the leaf, and our iniquities, like the wind, have taken us away. And there is none that calleth upon thy name, that stirreth up himself to take hold of thee; for thou*

13. According to Vergilius Ferm, in his *Encyclopedia of Religon*, published by the Philosophical Library in 1945, pages 511-2, the Attis worship became very popular around the same time as the birth of the Christian religion, and in the same places where Christianity developed. Frazer also points out that the religion of Attis worship took place in Syria, Rome and the vicinity.

14. Apparently, in honor of the supposed son of God, "Sun-day" became "Son-day"; however, the old name was retained.

hast hid thy face from us, and hast consumed us, because of our iniquities. But now, O Lord, thou art our father; we are the clay, and thou our potter, and we are all the work of thy hand. Be not wroth very sore, O Lord, neither remember iniquity for ever; behold, see, we beseech thee, we are all thy people." From this passage, as well as others such as Ecclesiastes (Kohelet) 7:20—*"For there is not a just man upon earth, that doeth good, and sinneth not—*the Christians have deduced that man is condemned to sin. Man must sin, and therefore, man needs something with which he can gain eternal salvation. That something, according to the Christians, is blood. Specifically, the blood of Jesus. The reason for this is because Leviticus 17:11 says that in order to achieve atonement, one needs blood. Let us therefore quote that passage as well: *"And whatsoever man there be of the house of Israel, or of the strangers that sojourn among you, that shall eat any manner of blood, I will set my face against that soul that eats blood, and will cut him off from among his people. For the life of the flesh is in the blood, and I have given it to you upon the altar to make an atonement for your souls: for it is the blood that maketh an atonement for the soul."* The Christians have seen from this that one needs blood in order to achieve atonement, and as Hebrews 9 points out, the blood of Jesus is the best blood possible. Thus, the death of Jesus, who supposedly died on the cross to atone for our sins, is the only way to achieve atonement. The argument is made even stronger, however, by the fact that, by looking at Isaiah 64:6 and Leviticus 17:11 together, you see that man is condemned to sin, and that man needs blood to atone for that sin, and now, after the destruction of the Temple, we cannot bring blood as an atonement to the Temple, and we are all therefore condemned to eternal damnation. However, God is merciful, and He would not allow all of mankind to be condemned to eternal damnation. He therefore died on the cross in order to atone for our sins. The missionaries will ask you—how can you achieve forgiveness today, if there is no Temple? Where you could offer blood?

This is one of the most fundamental issues of Christianity, and it is therefore very important to understand.

The first question that probably has already crossed your mind in that the timing is off. Jesus died around 32 A.D. and the Temple was destroyed in 70 A.D. If Jesus died in order to offer us a chance to atone for ourselves, because we need blood, then why did he die during the time when the Temple was still standing? Man did not need Jesus yet, so why did he die then? Did he die in advance?[15] Thus, this theory is incorrect, historically.

There are other problems, however, with their argument. Nowhere in the book of Leviticus, or anywhere else, does the Torah allow any form of human blood as an atonement. That was a purely pagan notion performed throughout the world, except in the Jewish world. The Jews have never offered a human sacrifice with the consent of the Jewish court and community. Furthermore, the entire chapter 17 of Leviticus, and even verse 11, seems to indicate in the strongest terms that all sacrifices and means for atonement that uses blood must be offered in the Tabernacle or the Temple. Since Jesus was not offered in the Temple, nor did any priest sprinkle his blood, he was not an atonement for anyone. In addition, the idea of a god dying in order to atone for the sins of others is also a pagan idea. See Frazer again, in the beginning of chapter 55, where he mentions that sometimes the accumulated sins of the entire people were placed upon their dying god. Frazer points out that this idea is basic to the pagan mind. In addition, the beginning of the book of Leviticus mentions various animals which could be used as an offering in the Temple, and since it specifies only certain animals, it indicates that only those

___

15. Should anyone answer this question by saying that Jesus was offering the people a last chance for forgiveness, then something is still very difficult, for Jesus should have been preaching a return to God and the Temple worship. Instead, he preached another message altogether—that we should accept Jesus as the Son of God. That was unnecessary, since the Temple was still standing. There was no need for the death of Jesus while the Temple still existed.

animals, and no other animals, and certainly no humans, may be used as an offering. See Lev. 1:2, 14. Since Jesus was certainly not an animal, he was disqualified. Lastly, Lev. 17:11 says that the blood must be on the altar, which did not take place in the case of the blood of Jesus.

Let us now deal with the issue of man and sin. Isaiah 64:6 was misunderstood or misinterpreted. The verse right before it says, among other things, the clause, "we have sinned." It is the beginning of a confession. The next verse then says that we are unclean, and our righteousness is as unclean as filthy rags. The Jews were confessing the reasons for the troubles that were besetting them, and they were saying that even the way that they did acts of righteousness were terrible. The commentaries point out that they felt proud when they acts of righteousness, or they did those acts for the sake of prestige and honor. Hence these acts were like dirty rags. The Jews were not saying, however, that whatever any person on earth does is like a dirty rag. That is openly contradicted by Deuteronomy 28, where it says that *"if you shall hearken diligently unto the voice of the Lord thy God, to observe and to do all His commandments which I command thee this day, then the Lord thy God will set thee on high above all nations of the earth. . .Blessed shalt thou be in the city, and blessed shall thou be in the field. Blessed shall be the fruit of thy body. . . blessed shall be thy basket and thy store. Blessed shall thou be when you come in, and blessed shall you be when you go out. . ."* See the entire passage for the list of all the blessings. Thus, God is saying that when you do the commandments properly, they will produce blessings of all sorts, not dirty rags. Look at Deuteronomy 30:8-14: *"And thou shalt return and obey the voice of the Lord, and do all His commandments which I command thee this day. And the Lord thy God will make thee plenteous in every work of thine hand, in the fruit of thy body, and in the fruit of thy cattle, and in the fruit of thy land, for good. . .If thou shalt hearken unto the voice of the Lord thy God, to keep His commandments and His statutes which are written in this book of the law, and if thou turn unto the Lord thy God with all thine heart, and with all thine soul. For this commandment which I command thee this day, it is not hidden from thee, nor is it far off. It is not in heaven, that thou should say, Who shall go up for us to heaven, and bring it unto us, that we may hear it, and do it? Neither is it beyond the sea, that thou should say, Who shall go over the sea for us, and bring it unto us, that we may hear it, and do it? But the word is very nigh unto thee, in thy mouth, and in thy heart, that thou may do it."* This is clearly saying that the command to hearken unto the word of God is near, it is accessible to the Jews, and all sorts of blessings will result from obeying those laws. This clearly is refuting the Christian claim that one is condemned to sin; it clearly is saying that we can obey the law, if we choose to do so. In fact, the next few verses continue and elaborate that: *"See, I have set before thee this day life and good, and death and evil. In that I command thee this day to love the Lord thy God, to walk in His ways, and to keep His commandments and His statutes and His judgements, that thou may live and multiply. . .therefore choose life. . ."* Thus, the Torah is most clearly saying that we have the control to deserve life, that we can be good enough to deserve divine blessing is our bodies, our crops, in all areas of our lives, as well as eternal life. Furthermore, this will result if we will choose to love God *and obey His commandments.* God said that the law is critical for our well being, unlike Paul, who claimed that it was not, in Galatians 3 and elsewhere. Thus, man is not condemned to sin, and we therefore do not need Jesus, or God, to die for our sins. That itself is a ridiculous concept. What good would it do for God to kill himself, as a means for my atonement? How will his death make me innocent? How can killing another vindicate my sins? Thus, that verse in Ecclesiastes must be understood to mean that nobody is perfect, in all probability. Man will probably sin, no matter what—but so what? God said that that will not deprive a person from blessing, because, as that verse in Deut. 30:8 said, *"And you shall return"*—if you return to God, i.e., even if you were away from God, even if you sinned, just return to Him, and then the Lord will place all types of blessings on you. Repentance is the key point, according to God. Thus, in Psalms 51:17, it says that *"The sacrifices of God are a broken spirit; a broken and contrite heart, O God, Thou wilt not despise."* Blood is not essential, Jesus is not essential, because God will always accept a broken, repentant spirit. Now we must come to another point which most people are unaware of. It seems that Psalms 51:17 seems to disagree with Lev. 17:11. The obvious answer is that in Leviticus, God is simply saying that He gave us the option of using blood, not that blood is essential. Thus, neither verse, nor any verse, will be saying that blood is essential.

If you look throughout the Bible, you will see more evidence of that. In Jonah 3:10, it says that *"God saw their works that they turned from their evil say"* and so He did not destroy the people of Nineveh. It says that God saw their change of behavior, not that He saw their blood offerings. In Hosea 14:2, in the original Hebrew, it reads, *"Return O Israel, unto the Lord your God, because you have stumbled in your sins. Take with you words, and return to the Lord; say unto Him, Forgive all of our iniquities and take the good (in us), and let our mouths pay, instead of bullocks."* The verse is clearly saying that a sincere return to God, with a verbal apology, is just as good as the blood of the bullocks. Thus, Ezekiel 33:11 says that God says *"that I have no pleasure in the death of the wicked, but that the wicked turn from his way and live. . ."* The main thing is to repent, turn from one's evil ways, and then one will live, and he will receive God's blessings, and he will be forgiven of all sin. That is the message of the Torah, if you read it honestly, and in the original Hebrew.

Thus, the notion that man is condemned to sin is not based on the Torah. The notion that we need blood, and blood alone, in order to receive forgiveness, is not based on the Torah.

Anyway, Jesus was not offered on the altar, he was not offered in the Temple, his blood was not sprinkled like all other offerings—in short, he was not a blood offering even if it would be possible to use humans, which, of course, is not permissible.

Thus, the Christians may ask you about Psalms 14:3 and perhaps other verses. Realize that they misunderstand those verses, or else the Bible is totally contradictory. Psalm 14:3, for example, says that God sees that no one does any good. This is referring to the fools of the first verse, where it explicitly says that there are no fools that do any good.

11. Isaiah 43:3—*"For I am the Lord thy God, the Holy One of Israel, thy Savior. . ."* The Christians learn from this that God will be the Messiah, because it says that that God is the Messiah. You may not understand what I am talking about, but the matter will become clear if you see the Hebrew. It says the word, "moshi-eh-cho," which sounds like the word, "Moshiach," which means Messiah. The trouble is that it is not the same word. The word in Hebrew, in this verse, comes from the word "Moshiah"—with the letter "Ayin" at the end of the word; the word thus means "savior." The word "Moshiach," with the letter "Ches" at the end, means an anointed one or a Messiah. Be careful of simple tricks like this which the missionaries love to pull on the unwary. Learn your Hebrew and you will have a lot of fun with the missionaries.

12. Genesis 18—Here are the relevant quotes: *"And the Lord appeared unto him (Abraham). . .and he lifted up his eyes and looked, and lo, three men stood by him, and when he saw them, he ran to meet them from the tent door, and bowed himself toward the ground. And said, My Lord, if now I have found favor in your sight, pass not away, I pray thee, from thy servant. Let a little water be fetched, I pray thee, and wash your feet. . ."* This passage has been used by missionaries to prove that God can and does make Himself corporal so that it would not be unusual to discover that God made Himself physically manifested in the body of Jesus. The proof is that God appeared as three men. Here is the sequence: the Lord appeared to Abraham; in what form? lo, in the form of three men. Then Abraham calls that group, Lord, or God. This shows that Abraham called the Trinity by the one name of God, and it shows that Abraham believed in the Trinity.

Of course, this is absurd, and again, based on an incorrect interpretation, due to a lack of the knowledge of Hebrew. In the Hebrew, verse 3 *(And said, My Lord. . .)* is in the singular. The next verse *(Let a little water. . .)* is in the plural. Thus, it is clear that verse 3 was addressed to God while the next verse was addressed to the three men. Abraham is asking God if He wouldn't mind waiting a bit while he took care of the three men. In no way at all is the verse saying that the three men are God personified. Thus, in verse 22, it says that *the men left* Abraham, *and the Lord was still there;* He was waiting for the men to leave. The Talmud[16] sees from this story that it is better to be hospitable than to talk to God Himself.

13. Psalm 2:7—Here are the relevant quotes, from the beginning of the Psalm: *"Why do the heathen rage, and the people imagine a vain thing? The kings of the earth set themselves, and the rulers take counsel together, against the Lord, and against his anointed, saying, Let us break their bands asunder, and cast away their cords from us. He that sits in the heavens shall laugh; the Lord shall have them in derision. Then He shall speak unto them in His wrath, and vex them in His displeasure. Yet I have set my king upon my holy hill of Zion; I will declare the decree: the Lord has said to me, you are my son, this day I have begotten you. Ask of me, and I shall give you the heathen for an inheritance, and the uttermost parts of the earth for your possession. You shall break them with a rod of iron, and dash them in pieces like a potter's vessel. Be wise, now, ye kings; be instructed, ye judged of the earth. Serve the Lord with fear, and rejoice with trembling. Kiss the son, lest he be angry and ye perish from the way, when his wrath is kindled but a little. Blessed are all they that put their trust in him."*

That is the entire Psalm 2, and, of course, the Christians say that the son referred to is Jesus. This, however, is not necessarily so, for the following reasons. Look at Psalm 89,

16. Shvuos 35b.

48

from verse 20 on, and you will see the following: *"I have found David my servant, with my holy oil have I anointed him. . . The enemy shall not exact from him, nor the son of wickedness afflict him, and I will beat down his foes before his face. . .He shall cry unto me, Thou art my Father, my God, and the rock of my salvation; also, I will make him my firstborn. . ."* Now, it is clear that David is being referred to as the son of God, for David will call God, "my Father," and God will call David, "my firstborn." Of course, this is metaphorical, but it is clear that Psalm 2 and 89 are parallels. Both discuss an anointed one, and in Psalm 89 it specifically states that it refers to David. Both mention that there will be no military problems. In addition, I doubt if Psalm 2 could even possibly refer to Jesus, since verse 8 would then be a problem: the son referred to there was to have control over the heathens, yet the heathen Romans controlled Jesus. To argue that it refers to the supposed second coming of Jesus is to force that into the verses, for you do not see any indications of two comings in Psalm 2. In addition, as it was pointed out before, the theory of the second coming is not based on Jewish tradition or sources, and is a theory born from desperation.

According to those Jewish commentaries which say that Psalm 2 refers to the Messiah specifically, and not David, that still leaves the issue open, for we still cannot know who the Messiah is. To say that Psalm 2 points necessarily and exclusively to Jesus, because he called himself the son of God, is really absurd, since all Jews are called the children of God in the Bible itself, in Deuteronomy 14:1.

Furthermore, there is an interesting mistranslation in the New Testament's version. In verse 12, they translate it as, "kiss the son." The only problem is that the word for "son" in the original is "bar," and "bar" means "son" in Aramaic, but not in Hebrew, and the Psalms (and all of Psalm 2) are all written in Hebrew.[17] That is why the Jewish commentaries

17. One must remember that King David lived hundreds of years before the Babylonian Exile, which is when the Jewish people first began to formally write in Aramaic.

translate it to mean "purity," and so the Psalm ends with an appeal that we serve the Lord with purity, not that we are to serve the son.

14. Isaiah 11:1, 2—Here are the quotes: *"And there shall come forth a rod out of the stem of Jesse, and a branch shall grow out of his roots; and the spirit of the Lord shall rest upon him, the spirit of wisdom and understanding, the spirit of counsel and might, the spirit of knowledge and the fear of the Lord."*

The Christians obviously understand that Isaiah is referring to Jesus. However, they have no evidence whatsoever that it really does refer to him. Simply because these verses refer to the Messiah, and they feel that Jesus is the Messiah, is not a proof at all. It is simply a claim, a conjecture. Furthermore, as Matthew 1 points out, Jesus did not come from Jesse (see page 36), and so these verses cannot refer to Jesus. Furthermore, if you look a mere four verses later, in Isaiah 11:6, Isaiah says that when this rod of Jesse appears, *"the wolf also shall dwell with the lamb, and the leopard shall lie down with the kid. . .and the lion shall eat straw like the ox. . .they shall not hurt nor destroy in all my holy mountain, for the earth shall be full of the knowledge of the Lord, as the waters cover the sea. And in that day there shall be a root of Jesse. . .and it shall come to pass in that day, that the Lord shall set His hand again the second time to recover the remnant of his people, which shall be left, from Assyria, and from Egypt. . . and shall gather the outcasts of Israel, and gather together the dispersed of Judah from the four corners of the earth. . ."*
These verses unquestionably do not refer to Jesus, for the wolves have not yet made peace with the lambs, the people of Israel and Judah have not been gathered yet from the four corners of the earth, let alone at the time of Jesus. In addition, the world is still not filled with the knowledge of the Lord. Thus, Isaiah 11:1-2 cannot refer to Jesus. Now, of course, the Christians may readily say that those verses refer to the second coming of Jesus, but if you look closely, even that becomes

very forced. This chapter seems to be divided into two parts: verses 1 to 9, and 9 to the end. Verse 1 refers to the rod of Jesse, and 9 again discusses the offspring of Jesse. The Christians claim that Isaiah 11:1, 2, 3, 4, and 5 definitely refer to Jesus. If so, it refers to his first coming, which they agree to (and verses 9 on would refer to this second coming). If that is the case, then the difficulty remains, for verses 6 to 9 discuss the wolf being friendly with the lamb and the whole world knowing God, which has not happened yet, on a real or symbolic level. Thus, the only hope for the Christian interpretation is to say, even though it is terriby forced, that verse 6 on refers to the second coming. If you see the entire context, however, you will see how forced this explanation is, especially since verse 9 and 10 both say, *"and in that* day"—which, by normal grammatical usage, would refer to some day previously mentioned, and more specifically, to the beginning of the chapter.

Thus, this chapter of Isaiah does not point to Jesus, and it seems to point to a descendant of Jesse, which disqualifies Jesus, according to Matthew 1. In addition, the prophecies of the chapter have not occurred yet, and the second coming theory is especially absurd in this particular concept.

15. Jeremiah 23:5—Here are the relevant quotes: *"Behold, the days come, saith the Lord, that I will raise unto David a righteous branch, and a king shall reign and prosper, and shall execute judgement and justice in the earth. In his days Judah shall be saved, and Israel shall dwell safely, and this is his name whereby he shall be called, The Lord Our Righteousness. Therefore, behold, the days come, saith the Lord, that they shall no more say, The Lord lives which brought the children of Israel out of the land of Egypt, but, The Lord lives which brought up and which led the seed of the house of Israel out of the north country, and from all countries which I have driven them, and they shall dwell in their own land."*

This passage, which supposedly refers to Jesus because of the reference to the branch of David, has all of the difficulties described in the "proof" mentioned before this one, plus some new ones. This passage has certainly not been fulfilled yet, for this branch of David shall be a reigning king, who shall execute justice, which Jesus did not fulfill. In the days of this branch, Judah and Israel shall be saved and will prosper. However, shortly after the death of Jesus, the second Temple and the Jewish state in Israel were destroyed. The name to be given to this branch of David was to be The Lord Our Righteousness, not Jesus, nor Yeshua, etc. The whole passage clearly has not occurred yet, nor does it point exclusively to Jesus, nor was Jesus from David. To claim that the entire passage refers to the second coming of Jesus is the same as admitting that it is no proof at all, because it is an admission that it does not refer to the first coming. Any passage which does not prove that Jesus, in his first coming, was the true Messiah, is meaningless, because one could just as well assume that it refers to whoever will turn out to be the real Messiah. Why assume that it refers to Jesus when almost all of the Jews at the time of Jesus rejected the idea that Jesus was the Messiah? If only the ignorant and the pagans liked the idea, why should anyone today, who is living 1900 years after the events, disagree with that vast majority who thought he was not a Messiah? The burden of proof always rests on the person or group which wishes to make a change in a status quo. Since Christianity is a supposed change or development of Judaism, according to Acts 10 and really, throughout the New Testament, as well as the early history of the church, the burden of proof rests upon the Christians. They are the ones who must show the legitimacy of their claims, and they must do by means of legitimate and solid proofs, not through nebulous and spurious allusions that could refer to a myriad of persons. Keep in mind that David lived around 900 years before Jesus, according to Jewish history and the Bible. That would allow for a vast number of children who would be eligible to become "branches" by the time of Jesus. Even then one would have to prove that he was the Messiah by means other than geneology alone. He would have to create peace for Judah and Israel, be a reigning king, gather the Jews from all the countries of the earth, etc.

Considering the fact that Jesus did *none* of these, and considering the fact that Matthew 1 says that Jesus was not from Joseph, and therefore not from David, it becomes almost incredible to accept Jesus as the Messiah (unless one needs to, for psychological reasons, but that is a different story altogether—I am dealing here with theological and historical truths, not neuroses).

16. Zechariah 9:9—This is the verse dealing with the Messiah coming on a donkey; this has already been discussed on pages 11-15. In addition, keep in mind that in the time of Jesus, riding on a donkey was not unusual at all. To say that since Jesus rode into Jerusalem on a donkey, that proves conclusively that he is the Messiah is totally absurd, considering the fact that there were probably thousands of other Jews on donkeys going to Jerusalem at the same time. It makes more sense to say that the verse refers to the 20th Century—while everyone else will fly to Jerusalem on a 747 jet, or drive a car, or ride in a bus or train, the Messiah will instead choose a donkey, which would be quite unusual. The main problems with this "proof," however, have been mentioned earlier; review them again, if necessary.

17. Isaiah 9:6—Here are the relevant quotes: *"The people that walked in darkness have seen a great light. . .For You have broken the yoke of his burden. . .the rod of his oppressor . . .For unto us, a child is born, unto us a son is given; and the government shall be upon his shoulder, and his name shall be called Wonderful, Counseller, The Mighty God, The everlasting Father, the Prince of Peace. Of the increase of his government and peace there shall be no end, upon the throne of David. . ."*

Missionaries feel that this verse also refers to Jesus, which really surprises me, because Jesus claimed to be the *Son* of God (John 10:33-38, 5:16-26; Matthew 16:13-17, etc.). He did not claim to be "God" Himself, nor did Jesus claim that He was the "Father," as Isaiah 9:6 claims. Furthermore, Jesus was *never called these names;* i.e., Wonderful, Prince of Peace, etc., even in the New Testament, and yet the verse says explicitly that the person referred to will be *called* those names.[18] Furthermore, in desperation, the Christians say that Isaiah 9:6 refers to Isaiah 7:14. The absurdity of 7:14 referring to Jesus has been discussed before on pages 38-41, and anyway, notice that the person in 7:14 was to be called Immanuel, which is not what the person in 9:6 is to be called. Why the difference in names, if it refers to the same person? And why wasn't Jesus called either of those names? Furthermore, 9:6 says that there will be no end of the government of this person, and no end to the peace. How can this refer to Jesus—his government never began, nor had any peace! If someone tells you that it refers to the second coming—well, by now, I think that you should be able to seek the weakness of that.

Thus, this verse refers to someone, but for sure not to Jesus, who was not called the Father, nor any of those names, nor had a government or peace.

18. Genesis 22:8—This verse is in the middle of the episode where God has commanded Abraham to offer his only son, Isaac, as an offering to God. On the way to the mountain, Isaac asks his father, *"Behold the fire and the wood, but where*

---

18. The missionaries may respond by saying that Jesus was described in the New Testament as doing marvelous, wonderful acts, and that he gave counsel, and talked of peace. That, however, is irrelevant, because Isaiah said that he would be *called* the name of Wonderful, Prince of Peace, etc. A name means a name, and Jesus was never called those names at all, even in the New Testament. He was called Jesus, Son of Man, etc., but never these names that Isaiah mentions here in 9:6.

Furthermore, the Hebrew does not really say that he will be called those names. It does not say "Vayeekorai" but rather, "Vayikra," which means, "he will call." Thus, many Jewish commentaries translate the verse like this: "And the Wonderful Counseler, the Mighty God, the Everlasting Father will call him (the boy that is born) the Prince of Peace." Thus, the verse does not say that the Prince of Peace will be another name for God. However, even this point is really superfluous, for Jesus was never called a Prince of peace, his government never began, etc.

is the lamb for a burnt offering? And Abraham said, my son, God will provide Himself a lamb for a burnt offering. . ."

From this passage, the Christians see something that amazed me when I first heard about it: just as Abraham offered his only son, so will God offer His only son. The problem with this insight, however, is that, first of all, it is based on a mistranslation. In the Hebrew original, it does not say that "God will provide Himself a lamb," which may indicate that God will offer Himself, or his son, as an offering (and note the amazing inherent paganism here—God might even kill Himself! or his son!? to atone for what? the sins of God??). If you see the original, in the Hebrew, it says that "God will show to Himself" ("yir-ah" means "to show, make another see"; "Lo" means "to him," not "himself"). Secondly, if you look a few verses later, one reads that God provided a ram for Abraham to slaughter instead of Isaac. Doesn't it make more sense to say that that ram is the animal referred to five verses earlier rather than saying that it refers to Jesus, 1500 years later? Furthermore, it does say a lamb in verse 8; that means a lamb, or ram, and as everyone agrees, Jesus did not appear to look like a furry lamb at all (although Jesus freaks do refer to Jesus as the Lamb—this verse is the origin of that name). Furthermore, the verse says, "a lamb," which seems to indicate nobody in particular. Had it said, "the lamb" or "my lamb," then perhaps their interpretation may have some basis (were it not for the other problems), but "a lamb" does not point to anyone at all. If you read the passage, the natural, straight message seems to have nothing to do with Jesus, a son of God, nor God's pet lamb either.

19. Exodus 12—In this passage, the Jews are commanded to kill a lamb before they leave Egypt, put the blood on the doorposts, and eat the lamb on the night before the Exodus. In verse 5, it says, *"your lamb shall be without blemish."* Verse 11 says, *"it is the Lord's passover,"* and verse 13 says, *"when I see the blood, I will pass over you, and the plague shall not be upon you to destroy you."*

By a manipulation of verses, and by taking everything out of context, the Christians deduced that Jesus was foreshadowed in the Pascal lamb, somehow, for he too, supposedly was perfect, and slaughtered (i.e., killed), and thereby supposedly atoned for us, for God saw his blood and therefore passed over us in His wrath.

This entire matter is ludicrous—read the entire passage and you will see that for yourself. Here are some of the difficulties with their interpretation. Verse 5 reads, in the entirety, *"Your lamb shall be without blemish, a male of the first year; you shall take it from the sheep, or from the goats."* Now, again, Jesus did not look like a sheep nor a goat. Verse 13 reads, in the entirety, *"And the blood shall be to you for a sign upon the houses where you are; and when I see the blood, I will pass over you, and the plague shall not be upon you to destroy you, when I smite the land of Egypt."* Note that last clause—when I smite the land of Egypt. Jesus had nothing to do with Egypt, so how could his verse refer to Jesus? This passage is only about the Pascal lamb, which like *any other offering* to God, cannot have a blemish, either (see Leviticus 22:17-25). The passage refers to a specific offering, which began in Egypt, and the blood was placed on the doorposts. Jesus had none of his blood placed on any doorposts. The meat had to be roasted (verse 8) and eaten (verse 8) and it had to be entirely consumed that night (verse 10); none of this seems to apply to Jesus—he was not roasted, nor eaten.

In short, unless one takes the entire passage out of context, and twists the words indiscriminately, this passage, in a normal, natural reading, has nothing to do with Jesus, or the death of any human.

20. Deuteronomy 6:4—*"Hear O Israel, the Lord our God, is one Lord."* This is the New Testament's translation, and the Christian understanding is that this verse teaches the truth of the Trinity, believe it or not! They point out that the verse mentions God three times, and concludes by saying it is all one. Thus, the Father, Son and Holy Ghost are all one, and the Shma[19] itself teaches that! Truly amazing—all of those Jews who died with the Shma on their lips, rather than convert to Christianity—incredible!

So let us examine the matter, let us look for the truth. If you go through the Torah in Hebrew, you will note that God seems to have various names. The two most frequent ones are the same two names which are in this verse. One name is based on the verb, "yeehyeh," which means "will be." This name refers to God as the source of existence, the Cause to Be. Since existence is the greatest good around, this name is also used to refer to God as God when He acts in a way which seems kind to man (such as a father who brings home a gift to his child). The other name, "Elohim"—which is in a plural form, indicates God as He acts in a plurality. When the world seems to have a God of good and God of evil at the same time, there the Torah will use Elohim. Thus, this name is used to refer to God as the God of justice[20] (such as the father who spanks the child who threw a knife at his kid brother). That is the basics of how classical Judaism has always understood these names. Thus, the basic Jewish understanding of the Shma has been: Listen, Jews, God, who acts (sometimes) like a multi-faceted God to us, is really one God (He is really pure unity in essence). Rashi, the famous medieval commentary on the Bible and the Talmud, has a different translation: Listen Jews—God, who is presently our God—He is accepted by the Jews—should become One God. (He should become accepted by the entire world, there should be no other gods accepted by mankind, and the Jews are to effect this change). Both of these translations fit into the words. The Christian interpretation, however, does not fit into the words. If the Shma refers to the Father, and the Son, and the Holy Ghost, then there should be *three* different names in the Shma. Instead, there are only *two*, for the first and

---

19. The "Shma" is the term that is often used by the Jewish people when referring to this passage, since the passage begins with the Hebrew word, "Shma" (Hear, listen).

20. In other words, the God of reward and punishment (justice) seems to be a plurality, since both reward and punishment, which seem to be opposites, are from the one God.

the third are the same name. It makes no sense whatsoever to say that the Father is equal to the son and the Holy Ghost, and yet call them different names, unless all three names are equal, or all three are different. Since the Jews, whom this verse is directed to, always, throughout their history, understood this verse to mean that God is one, He has no partners, sons or virgin wives, and since the Christian translation does not fit into the words, it is clear that the Christian interpretation is not the correct one. In a similar analysis, the Christian "proof" from Genesis 1:26—*"Elohim said, Let us. . ."* is easily disproven by the next verse, which says that Elohim created (in the singular) man in *His* image. Thus, in verse 26, God was obviously talking to other beings, such as angels, but—only God, in the singular, did the creating.

21. Isaiah 48:12-16—Here are the quotes: *"Hearken unto me, O Jacob and Israel, my called; I am he, I am the first, I also am the last. My hand has also laid the foundation of the earth, and my right hand has spanned the heavens; when I call unto them, they stand up together. All you, assembly yourselves, and hear; which among them has declared these things? The Lord has loved him, He will do his pleasure on Babylon, and His arm shall be on the Chaldeans. Even I have spoken; yea, I have called him; I have brought him, and he shall make his way prosperous. Come you near unto me, hear this: I have not spoken in secret from the begining; from the time that it was, there I am; and now the Lord God, and His Spirit, have sent me."*

Missionaries see the Trinity in this passage, because it starts off discussing the creator of the world, and in the last verse, it adds the Spirit, plus "me." In order words, and from a different angle, it starts off with an "I" who refers to himself as the creator, and this creator ends his speech by saying that the "Lord God" and the "Spirit" have sent "me"—the me being the same person as the I mentioned before, namely, the creator. So there are three beings mentioned: I, or me, who is the creator; the Lord God; and the Spirit. Thus, Isaiah believes in the Trinity, and so should we, according to the Christians.

Of course, by now you would expect some basic flaw in the "proof" and, of course, there is. If you simply read the *very next verse* that follows the above quote, you will find, *"Thus saith the Lord, they Redeemer, the Holy One of Israel; I am the Lord thy God which teaches you to derive benefit..."* Note those words, "Thus saith the Lord"—they are always used to introduce a prophetic message. See Isaiah 43:1; 45:1; 56:1; 66:1, etc. This means that the verse beginning with, "Thus saith..." is the message of the prophet—that is Isaiah talking. So if verse 17 is Isaiah talking, it seems likely that the *previous* verse would introduce this prophetic message. Thus, if you look at the entire chapter of 48, you will see three prophetic messages: verse 1 begins with, *"Hear ye this..."*; verse 12 begins with, *"Hearken unto me..."*; verse 17 begins with, *"Thus saith the Lord..."* There are three groups, but note that the first two begin the same way, so one could assume that the third is somewhat separate in essence or time span. Because of this, the Jewish commentaries understand that the last verse of the second series introduces, with a little introduction, the third message. Thus, when Isaiah says that "and now the Lord God and His Spirit have sent me," the "me" refers to Isaiah. *Isaiah* is saying, God has now sent me, and here is His message: Thus saith the Lord...

A proof to this is that if the Christians were consistent, then there are more than three parts to God, for in the whole chapter that these verses are found, chapter 48, God is referred to as *"the Lord of Hosts"* (verse 2), *"the Lord"* (verse 14), *"the Lord God"* (verse 16), *"Spirit"* (verse 16), the *"Redeemer"* (verse 17), and *"the Holy One of Israel"* (verse 17). This adds up to a total of *six* names. Thus, one should deduce, if the Christians are intellectually honest and consistent, that there are six parts to God, not three. However, even they do not accept this.

There is one other problem with this "proof." According to the myopic vision of the Christians, there are three names—the Creator, the Lord God, and the Spirit. So which one is Jesus? The Trinity consists of the Father, the Son, and the Holy

Ghost (Matthew 28:19). The Spirit is the same as the Holy Ghost, according to the Christians. So, in Isaiah 48, either the Creator or the Lord God is Jesus—which one is it? To say that Jesus is the creator of the world is to disagree with John 1:1-5, 18; 5:18-23, etc., which states that God created the world, Jesus is His son, and the son derives his authority from the father. See John 15:1, 5: *"I (Jesus) am the true vine, and my Father is the husbandman. . .I am the vine, and you are the branches."* God is the cultivator, the planter—i.e., the creator. Thus, Jesus must be the being referred to as "the Lord God"— which is unusual, to say the least, because Jesus is never referred to as the "Lord God," and Jesus is never referred to as "God" either. In the New Testament, "God" always refers to the Father (see, for example, John 8:42). Thus, Isaiah 48 seems to explicitly exclude Jesus, even if it were to include a trinity!

22. Psalm 118:22—*"The stone which the builders refused is become the head stone of the corner."*

The Christians see Jesus as the refused stone who became the head. Their proof is simply because Jesus was disrespected by all of his people, and then made the head of a religion by the pagan, ignorant Gentiles in the neighborhood. Of course, this proof is invalid, for, first of all, this verse does not prove anything, or assert anything. If you see the context, it is part of an expression of thanks, not in the middle of a prophecy. Second, using the same reasoning of the Christians, one could say that this verse refers to Adolf Hitler, for he too was refused power in the 1920's and then became the head stone of the world. Or, it could refer to King David, himself, the author of this Psalm, who was refused an interview when his brothers were interviewed for the position of King of Israel (see 1 Samuel 16:1-12). In short, this verse does not point exclusively and necessarily to Jesus, and the context of the verse seems to exclude it from being a prophecy altogether.

23. Psalm 69:21—*"They also gave me gall for my meat, and in my thirst they gave me vinegar to drink."*

Supposedly this refers to Jesus, who was given vinegar to drink while he was crucified. Of course, if you look at the entire Psalm, it is obviously not referring to Jesus. There are verses that say, "O God, thou knowest my foolishness, and my sins are not hid from thee." The Christians claim that Jesus never sinned, yet the subject of this Psalm claimed that he did sin. Furthermore, all of these verses in the Psalm could easily refer to David, while he was hiding from King Saul. Better yet, they could refer to the Jewish people on the whole, for the verses say that there are many who "hate me without cause." This applies to the Jews, but not so much to Jesus, for the Jews had a reason why they did not accept Jesus, and the New Testament quotes their reasons—see John 5:16, 18; 8:33-58, etc. It says in this Psalm that *"I made sackcloth my garment."* This is true of the Jewish people, but there is no reference at all for Jesus wearing a sackcloth. In short, this chapter does not point exclusively, nor preferably, to Jesus.

24. Zechariah 11—This is a very difficult passage of the Bible; look it up, read it, and you will see that it is a very vague passage. In the middle of the chapter, Zechariah says, in the name of God, *"And I took my staff, even Beauty, and cut it asunder, that I might break my covenant which I had made with all of the people. And it was broken in that day, and so the poor of the flock that waited upon me knew that it was the word of the Lord. And I said unto them, If you think good, give me my price; and if not, forbear. So they weighed for my price thirty pieces of silver. . ."*

The Christians see this as a prophecy that foretells the thirty pieces of silver that was paid to Judas in order that he would betray Jesus and turn Jesus in to the Romans (Matthew 26:14-16). The problem with this interpretation is that the words of Zechariah have been twisted to mean the very opposite of their intended meaning. Zechariah says that the poor who waited upon God—which must mean the righteous people—were told by God, that if they think good—that means, if they wish to be righteous—then they should give a price (whatever that means)—and they did so. Thus, the poor, who waited upon the Lord, did that which was *good*, and weighed out thirty pieces of silver. Zechariah calls that an act of goodness, and yet, somehow, the Christians twisted it to refer to an *evil* act of betrayal. Thus, whatever this passage means, it clearly says that the payment was a good thing, and that is all that is need to see the falseness of the "proof." Besides that, reread pages 26 and 27; do not forget that there is a great probability that the Christian story has been doctored so that the Jesus story seems to reflect Old Testament prophecies.

25. Genesis 49:10—*"The sceptre shall not depart from Judah, nor a lawgiver from between his feet, until Shiloh shall come. . ."* Since many of the Jewish commentators translate or explain Shiloh to mean the Messiah, the verse is prophesying that the Messiah will come *before* the sceptre is taken from Judah. Since the second Jewish commonwealth, with its kings, ended in 70 A.D.,it is clear that the Messiah should already have come. Since Jesus was the only person who claimed to be the Messiah, before 70 A.D., and the sceptre was removed shortly afterwards, it is clear that Jesus is the Messiah. This is how the Christians see the matter.

The problem with that interpretation is very obvious to anyone who knows Jewish history. If you study this history of the Jews, you will see that the last Jewish king *from the tribe of Judah* reigned at the end of the first Temple, after which he was carried off into exile (2 Kings 24:12-20; 25:1-11). *None* of the kings during the period of the second Temple were from the tribe of Judah. In the beginning of the period of the second Temple, the high priest was the political leader (he was from the tribe of Levi), then the family of the Maccabbees took over, who were also from the priestly family, and then Herod took over. He was not from Jewish blood altogether. Thus, if Jesus is the person referred to, it seems strange that he came hundreds of years *after* the secptre departed from Judah.

Thus, if you know or read your Jewish history, it is quite clear that the sceptre did depart from Judah *before* Jesus came, and so the verse is not referring to him. The verse is basically saying that the Jewish people *should not* remove the sceptre from the tribe of Judah, and give it to a member of another tribe. During the second Temple, when the Maccabbees took the sceptre, they violated this law, and thereby brought disaster upon the Jewish people.[21] This verse is a command, not a prophecy, as we can see from Jewish history.

By now, I am sure, you see the type of "proofs" used by the missionaries, and the method of analyzing those "proofs." There are other "proofs" which the missionaries have, but the above are their main ones, or, at least, their most popular ones. The main thing is to understand the method of analysis and calmly apply it to any other quote that may be shown you. Always check the Hebrew, but as you may have noticed, that often will be unnecessary, for the text itself, with a little common sense, will be adequate.

After all of the above, however, you will probably be bothered by an enormous question. If their proofs to the divinity of Jesus are really that poor, and that they really have no proof whatsoever that Jesus is the son of God, who will atone for man, then why do so many Christians believe in Christianity? True, the Jews saw the absolute absence of any proof, but what convinced the Christians? Can all of those millions of people be wrong? This question, in itself, is used by the Christians as another proof; and, indeed, what is the answer?

The answer is really simple. Christianity may be utter nonsense, from a *theological* and *historical* point of view, but, *psychologically*, it is tremendous. It offers man a world to come, eternal happiness, with very little effort. A good Christian goes to church once a week, doesn't steal or commit adultery or murder (unless it is in the name of the Church, such as during the Crusades), puts a little money in the collection plate on Sunday, and presto! he gets eternal happiness. That is a rather cheap price to pay for such bliss. Thus, even though

21. See the commentary of Nachmanides on Genesis 49:10.

many Christians have not thought about their religion, and many do not know or read the Bible (and remember, a Christian must read only the Bible, with no commentaries, while a Jew should read the Bible, with the commentaries, the vast Talmud, with its commentaries, the complicated codes of law, etc.), they believe in Jesus, for that is the one price you must pay to be a Christian—you must forfeit your brain and intellectual honesty. The Jewish people died at the stake rather than pay that price, but then, not everyone is willing to pay the price that it takes to be a good Jew. The Jew must study every spare moment he has, he must try to always do acts of charity, he must eat only certain foods, and cannot work on the Sabbath, etc. Of course, many Jews today have chosen to act non-Jewish, but that is the very point. To be Jew requires a lot of commitment; to be a Christian requires only faith—and when eternal bliss is waved before one's eyes, it is easy to believe in anything.

It may be worth while for you to reread page 11, in the Introduction, regarding the psychological motives for becoming a Christian. If you keep your eyes open, you will see a great many Christians who accepted Jesus in a time of crisis. Always ask them why they become a Christian, and you will usually find a crisis in their lives.

In addition to the above psychological motivations for becoming a Christian, there is another very powerful one. It is based on the feeling of guilt that all of us have. Most of us have done some evil things in our lives, and some of us have done some very terrible things. As a result, most people walk around with a deep sense of guilt, which means that deep down, they are miserable and uncomfortable. They feel ugly, sinful, and evil. To this, the Christians come with their unique message. They claim that nobody is evil, nobody is ugly, because Jesus has forgiven everybody. One can be a prostitute like Mary, and be beloved by God, simply by accepting Jesus in your heart. That again is a very cheap price to pay in order to look and feel beautiful, inside, where it really counts. The Jew is told that if he did do something evil, he must repent sincerely before

God—but that means that one must sincerely repent. The Christian, or non-Jew, seems to find that too difficult, and would rather worship a man, hanging on the wall with his arms stretched out, before he would sincerely repent. Perhaps this explanation will help you understand the Christian neurosis with sin, and hell. Jesus freaks will hand out literature with *"HELL"* written in huge letters, and solemnly warn you that unless you accept Jesus, that is where you will go. There is a total obsession with hell and guilt, and the reason is because they know that that is the primary reason why most people are interested in Christianity. Man seeks eternal happiness for a cheap price. Man wants to avoid hell, which he has been led to believe waits for him, for as cheap a price as he can negotiate. The true Christian is often simply another Faust, who also sold his soul to the devil for an enjoyable, neurosis free, guilt-free life on earth.[22]

Before we conclude this section, there is one more "proof" that should be mentioned, and it incorporates both the psychology as well as the guilt that was mentioned above. Some Christians may tell you that the Christian story must be true, for if it were not, then why were those Christian martyrs willing to face the lions of the Romans rather than renounce their faith. Some-

22. You must realize that when you discover the psychological need or problem in a person which caused him or her to accept Jesus, you may be opening up a Pandora's box which may require professional help to close. That, however, is the point—Christianity is the panacea for the sorry soul, but it is not truth. Some turn to drugs, others to alcohol, and others to Jesus—it's all the same thing. If you are really trying to help that person achieve a permanent, psychologically healthy state of being, be prepared to substitute an honest, true substitute for Jesus. You should not simply destroy Jesus and then leave them in a psychological vacuum. If you ask, this book tries to do just that, my answer is that my own hopes are that the Jewish reader will come to appreciate Judaism, after studying all the texts. Classical Judaism, which does not abrogate every law which seems incongruous with modern America, is emotionally, theologically, and historically solid, if you study it well, and with the primary sources, including the Talmud. My hopes are that the person will come to appreciate the study of truth, even if that person may feel that Judaism is not the truth. Once a person is interested in truth, real truth, then that person will find the truth, and that will fill up any psychological vacuum. That has been the purpose of this book—to show how to see truth, to critically analyze the basis for the system of belief called Christianity, and to perhaps interest the reader into looking for the truth, wherever it may be found.

thing must have convinced them of the veracity of the Christian story—it was good enough for them to give up their lives for it—and whatever it was, it should be good enough for us.

If you think about it, however, this "proof" is as bad as the rest of theirs. First of all, it ignores history. The early Moslems, in the 600's, were willing to give up their lives for their beliefs. The Jews, in the year 1096, and afterwards during the Crusades, were also willing to give up their lives for their beliefs. Thus, the willingness to give up one's life instead of one's beliefs does not prove a theological truth, because the Christian will say that the Moslem and the Jew are theologically incorrect, yet both gave up their lives rather than their beliefs. Thus, just because the Christian also gave up his life rather than his belief does not prove that Christianity is the truth. If it were a good proof, then it proves that all three religions are true, and the Christian will deny that. So, either the willingness to give up one's life proves that all three are correct, or else, it proves nothing at all regarding the truth of any belief.

The truth is, as the above proves, that a willingness to give up one's life rather than one's belief proves nothing, except that that person himself thought that his belief was absolutely true. But just because you think that you are right, does not make you right. People risk their fortunes on investments which they are positively certain about, and yet learn, to their dismay, that certitude does not equal reality. Certitude, confidence, faith—all these do not create reality, nor do they necessarily coincide with reality. People discover that their most basic axioms are sometimes wrong, even though they were positive about it. People thought the earth was flat, they were certain—and they were wrong. The Church excommunicated those who thought that the earth revolved around the sun—and the Church was wrong. People trust their wives, husbands or friends—and discover that they were wrong for doing so, even though they trusted them with even their lives. People will give up their lives for political causes, people will risk their lives for prestige, people will risk their lives for a wide variety of reasons. This has happened throughout history, and quite often, those people discovered that they incorrectly thought that they possessed absolute truth.

Thus, this last "proof" is not justified from both a psychological as well as historical perspective—but notice the attempt to use guilt as a means of persuasion. Christianity thrives on guilty feelings, promises of eternal bliss, etc., but not on truth.

SECTION TWO

Here are some questions which help point out the problems with Christianity on the whole. The first group of questions, which will be numbered A1, A2, A3, etc., will deal with problems with Christianity from a historical point of view. The second group, which will numbered B1, B2, etc., will deal with Christianity from a theological point of view.

A1. As history and Acts 13:46 demonstrate, the Jewish people, on the whole, rejected the divinity of Jesus—why did they reject him? Why should someone today believe in the divinity of Jesus when his own countrymen, his own fellow Jews, did not believe in it? How could we know more about Jesus today, after 1900 years, than the people in his own generation? After all, when it comes to history, the more primary the source, the more authoritative it is, and so why accept he whom the Jews rejected? In fact, the New Testament was written originally in Greek, even though Jesus was a Jew who probably spoke Hebrew as his native language, and all of the apostles were Hebrew speaking Jews. This shows the strong antipathy which the Jewish people felt towards the whole idea. As Gibbon, in his famous history of the Roman Empire, points out, the Jews in Israel found it unnecessary to publish or at least preserve any Hebrew text of the New Testament.[1] So why accept Jesus if the vast majority of his own people rejected him?

Some missionaries answer this by saying that the Jews were all stupid. As anyone knows, after studying a bit of the Talmud, which was studied in the time of Jesus, many of the Jews were brilliant, not stupid. Furthermore, if you read the arguments by the Jews themselves, in the New Testament, you will see that they were certainly not stupid. See John 6 and 8; would your reaction be any different than that of those Jews? Furthermore, while all of the non-Jews in Europe at the time, and in the Middle East, were illiterate, almost all of the Jews were literate, thinking people. (This pattern continued through the Middle Ages—the Jews were always literate, even when their neighbors were not.) To call the Jews stupid, and the pagans smart, is to ignore the history and facts about the two groups.[2]

A2. Why should anyone believe in the supposed resurrection of Jesus when some of the apostles themselves did not believe it? If you look in the last chapter of Matthew, the claim is made that Jesus arose from the dead, and the apostles went to meet him. Verse 17 then says, *"And when they saw him, they worshipped him, but some of them doubted."* So why shouldn't all of us doubt; we were not even his disciples?

A3. If Jesus really did return from the dead, and if he really came in the name of grace and kindness, then why

1. Edward Gibbon, *Christianity and the Decline of Rome* (an abridgment of the first part of *The Decline and Fall of the Roman Empire*), The Macmillan Co., 1966, page 133.

2. In fact, Paul himself, who, in Romans 9:30-33 gives the poorest answer (the Jews denied Jesus because they did not have faith, which is a totally circular argument), also did not originally believe in Jesus. Paul, himself, the author of most of the New Testament, used to go around killing Christians! (See Acts 8:1, 3; 9:1; 13:9.) It took a supposed revelation from heaven (Acts 9:3) to convince Paul. If it needed that much to persuade him, and not solid theological or historical proofs, it is ony fair to state that without any similar revelation, it is foolish to accept Jesus. The Jews were being only as smart as Paul was, not a bit less.

didn't he reveal himself to everyone? In the last chapter of Matthew, for example, Jesus reveals himself to only two women and eleven disciples—why so few? If eternal bliss depends on faith in Jesus, why didn't he make this bliss more accessible by showing more people that he in fact was resurrected?

The true answer seems to be very simple. The resurrection story is a fabricated hoax; it never happened. However, those early followers just could not believe that their savior just simply died and was no more. They wanted to make Jesus into a god—they needed to make Jesus a god. They therefore made up a story (maybe it was a hallucination which they thought was true) and the story that they made up was one that could not be disproven. If someone claims that a Martian came and spoke with him for an hour in his living room, that cannot be disproven; it is either believed or disbelieved. Had the Christians claimed that Jesus arose from the dead and walked all over the Galilee, or walked throughout Jerusalem, then, of course, the hoax would immediately be seen as a lie, if, in fact, there was no resurrection. So the question remains—why did Jesus stay incognito after the supposed resurrection, according to the version of the Gospels? If you say that he wanted to make belief in Jesus difficult, then why did Jesus exert so much effort *before* the cruicifixion trying to convince people of his divinity and ability to effect salvation? So that cannot be the reason. The only likely reality is that he never survived the crucifixion, but his followers could not accept that psychologically, and so they made a god out of Jesus, just as the followers of Buddha made a god out of him after his death. Once the Christians made a god out of Jesus, they had to create a story that would be befitting a god. They therefore took the pagan myths that were prevalent in the area, saw that the theme of resurrection was appropriate, and so, they claimed that Jesus also must have resurrected himself. They were in enough control of their imagination, however, to limit their story to unverifiable limits, so that their report could not be tested and proven to be true. Deep down, they too knew it was not true.

If this theory is not correct, why didn't Jesus reveal himself to more than a tiny group of people?

A4. If God gave the law in front of the entire nation of Israel, then shouldn't God have abrogated it also in front of the entire nation? As Exodus 19 explicitily points out, the entire nation was present when God gave the Torah to the Jewish people at Mount Sinai. Now, if the Christian claim is correct that the laws of the Torah no longer need to be obeyed, because Jesus fulfilled them for us, then wouldn't it make sense for God to cancel his original commands in the same manner that He gave them—i.e., in front of all the people. Wouldn't it be peculiar if the President of the United States made a new decree, and proclaimed it on prime time on TV and radio, and then, a few years later, *after no indication whatsoever*, let his press secretary quietly tell a few people that the law need no longer to be obeyed? There was no indication at all among the Jews that Torah law need no longer be obeyed, and all of a sudden, for reasons which we will discuss soon, the word was spread by the followers of Jesus that the Torah need no longer be obeyed. Does this make sense?

A5. Why did the Romans put the words, "King of the Jews" on the head of Jesus when he was crucified? That is what it says in Matthew 27:37, and it implies that the Romans killed Jesus for political crimes, not religious crimes. Furthermore, if the New Testament is correct in its story that the Jews turned Jesus into the Romans, then it becomes very difficult to understand. If the Jews turned him in, then they obviously did not like Jesus, so why would the Romans call him the King of the Jews right after the Jews turned Jesus in to the Romans? Something is obviously mixed up—the story was written by a poor reporter, or else by a fabricator who did not like Jews. It is totally contradictory to write that Pontius Pilate thought that Jesus was blameless, and then write that Pilate accused Jesus of being King of the Jews, in a derogatory fashion, when it was clear to all that the Jews did not accept him as a king. So if the Gospels are correct, why did the Romans place that sign over

Jesus? Lastly, why didn't Pilate pardon Jesus if he thought that Jesus was innocent? He certainly had the authority to do so, and, according to historians, he certainly was not afraid of the Jews.[3] Thus, how can the Gospels be reconciled with the history?

A6. If Christianity is the religion of grace, brotherly kindness, and other nice qualities, as the Christians claim it is, then why have the Christians throughout history been so cruel and murderous, especially towards the Jews? If you would read, *The History of Anti-Semitism* by Leon Poliakov, and the book by Malcolm Hay, published under the titles of either *The Foot of Pride* or *Europe and the Jews*, you would see some shocking evidence of Christian behavior throughout the centuries. Here are some examples from the two books. It was the annual custom at Toulouse to drag a Jew into the Church of St. Stephen and slap him on the face before the altar, occasionally with such force that, at least once, the Jew's brains and eyes were knocked out.[4] During the Crusades, starting in 1096, many non-Jewish history books fail to point out that thousands of Jews were offered the cross or the sword,[5] and so, thousands of Jews were killed throughout France and Germany. The Crusaders themselves were promised eternal happiness by the Church for killing "infidels" such as the Jews.[6] In 1215, at the Fourth Lateran Council, Pope Innocent

---

3. Some Christians have made the claim that since Pilate did so many other evil deeds, he was in trouble with Rome, and he therefore was nervous about his job, and was therefore afraid of the Jews. This is totally unsubstantiated from the history of the times, and Josephus strongly implies the very opposite. Pilate was ruthless, and not afraid of the Jews at all. One thing everyone, except the New Testament, agrees upon—Pilate was a cruel, evil man. The New Testament twisted this fact, and has tried to lead people into believing that Pilate was a nice, gentle fellow who loved truth and justice. That is an absolute falsehood.

4. Malcolm Hay, *Europe and the Jews*, Boston, Beacon Press, 1961, pages 36-7.

5. See Edward Flannery, *The Anguish of the Jews*, New York, 1965, in the Introduction on page xi. This book is an excellent summary of Christian anti-Semitism, and the unique thing about it is that it was written by a Catholic priest.

6. Leòn Poliakov, *The History of Anti-Semitism*, New York, New York, Schocken Books, 1974, all of chapter four.

III decreed that Jews in Christian countries must wear something that easily reveals them to be Jews. Jews were forced to wear yellow circular forms, pointed hats, and similar disgracing items when they were in public.[7] Hitler learned this piece of history well, and revived this Christian custom when he took control over Nazi Germany. If you read *A History of the Marranos* by Cecil Roth, you will see what Christian "love" is about, in its true form. Roth describes the procedures of the Holy Inquisition in Spain, where, after totally secret trails, various tortures might be used to elicit from the accused a confession that the person had been doing Jewish practices. In the earlier period, the most common torture would be to raise the accused, and then let him fall from a beam, to which he was attached to by a short rope, so that when he fell, he would stop with a horrible jerk before he reached the ground. This would be done by tying the accused person's hands behind his back, and with weights tied to his legs. As you can see, doing this a few times would disjoint, if not break, one's arms, and possibly legs as well. This, as well as the other tortures, were done on women, too. If that did not work, the kind inquisitors would lay the accused on their backs, place a wet cloth on the nostrils and mouth, and have a trickle of water constantly poured into the throat. The person would constantly gag, as well as suck the cloth into the throat, which would periodically be suddenly removed—this would pull with it both water and blood, and be terribly painful. Another favorite torture would be to tie a rope around one's arm or leg, and keep tightening that rope until the person confessed, or the rope went to the bone, or the rope broke. To deserve this gift of Christian love, one had to be a Christian who was accused of doing anything Jewish at all, even putting out new linen on Friday afternoon. If you ask, this was not anti-Semitic at all— it was only against the Christians—then you must realize that in 1391, Archdeacon Ferrand Martinez went throughout Spain, offering Jews the sword or the cross. Many accepted the

7. Ibid, pages 64 to 67.

cross in order to save their lives. In 1411, another Christian cleric called Ferrer did it again. Thus, there were at least 50,000 (some say many more) Jews who accepted Christianity instead of the sword, and it was these pseudo-Christians, who were called Marranos ("pigs" in Spanish), who were watched most carefully by the Holy Inquisition. So first the church offered the sword or the church. If one accepted the church, then, after any slightly Jewish action, the above tortures went into effect. If the accused confessed, or was considered guilty, then the person would be punished severely, quite often by being burned alive at the stake. However, if the person repented of his sin, then Christian "mercy" would go into effect—the person would be strangled before being burned at the stake.[8]

All of the above examples were done with the consent of the Church. (The Christian peasants have done other evils to the Jews, but since the Church did not authorize them, I did not discuss them.[9]) So the official policy of Christiandom accepted the above tortures, forced conversions, slaughter of those who did not wish to convert, etc. Thus, the question could be asked—has there been a religion more cruel than Christianity? How could anyone who knows history expect that the belief in Jesus will make him kind or gentle?

Many Christians will say that those Christians who did those terrible things acted in a very un-Christian like manner. But that is ridiculous since they did them all in the name of Jesus.[10] They thought that that was the very thing that Jesus

8. Cecil Roth, *A History of the Marranos*, Meridian Books, 1960, chapters one and five.

9. The Church has done other evils, such as force the Jews into ghettoes, which were cramped quarters in the worst part of town, from which the Jews were not allowed to leave at night. One of the worst ones was the ghetto of Rome, which was instituted by Pope Paul IV in 1556—read *The Ghetto and the Jews of Rome* by Ferdinand Gregorovius. However, at least they did not kill Jews outright in the ghettoes, as they did in the other situations which were mentioned.

10. In addition, they were usually initiated by the popes themselves, which, at that time, represented *all* of the Christian people. Thus, it was Pope Urban II who initiated the Crusades in 1096, the Inquisition was initiated by Gregory IX, and the Roman ghetto by Paul IV.

would like them to do; that was the accepted interpretation of Christianity. If today's Christians feel that it was a misinterpretation, then the question is—who is the offical arbiter of Christian truth? At least in those days, all of the Christians agreed that it was a Christian thing to do. Is there such unity today? And even in modern times, during the Nazi destruction of the Jews, the Pope remained silent the entire time, even when he knew what was happening and could have done something (read *The Deputy* by Rolf Hochhuth). This silence were perfectly consistent with the essence of the Christian attitude towards the Jews throughout history—either convert them, or kill them, or watch them be killed.

So the question remains—why were the Christians so terribly cruel to the Jews and how could one call Christianity a religion of love, when so many people have been murdered in the name of Jesus?

A7. Since even the Christians agree that Jesus did not fulfill most of the Old Testament prophecies about the Messiah, then why should anyone accept Jesus as the Messiah? Jesus has hardly fulfilled any of the prophecies, and the only ones that he did fulfill were just very general ones such as the fact that he rode on a donkey, or that he suffered, which thousands of other Jews did as well. The donkey was the basic mode of transportation, and the Jews were often killed brutally, or crucified, by the Romans, around the time of Jesus. So Jesus fulfilled nothing that was unique. The *key* prophecies, however, were *unfulfilled* by Jesus. He did not fulfill the prophecy of gathering all of the twelve tribes together from around the world (Ezekiel 37). Jesus did not fulfill the prophecy which said that after the Messiah comes, the entire world will worhip only the one God (Isaiah 11, Zechariah 14). He did not fulfill the prophecy that peace would reign throughout the world, and that swords would be beaten into plowshares (Isaiah 2). The prophecy that all of the world will call Jerusalem the throne of the Lord, and the nations of the world will no longer walk after the imagination of their evil hearts

(Jeremiah 3) has still not been fulfilled. The gathering of all of the Jews into their own land, and the grant of a new heart and spirit into the Jews, and the absence of famine, and the great increase in the fruit of the land (Ezekiel 36)—none of these have been fulfilled.

Since the main prophecies were not fulfilled by Jesus, and only such prophecies such as riding on a donkey, or getting beaten up were fulfilled by him, why should one believe that Jesus was the Messiah?

******

B1. How can three equal one? The Trinity is one of the most difficult concepts in Christianity, and they themselves do not thoroughly understand it. As you know, three apples of equal size do not weigh the same as one of those apples. Three people cannot sit on a chair which seats only one. Yet the Christians feel that there can be three separate gods who are really one. This is not a matter of theological profundity, but rather, illogical thinking which no thinking person should accept. Three can never equal one. Either there are three gods, or there is only one, but it cannot be both. If Jesus is separate from the Father (and the Christians say that he is), then he is separate from Him. Jesus cannot be separate and not separate at the same time, just as no other being could be honestly considered to exist and not exist at the same time. The reason for this absurd doctrine, is, I'm sure, again because of the difficult circumstances which the early Christians had to live through. They thought that Jesus was a god, and they also accepted God as their god. It then occurred to them that either God is God, or Jesus is God, but how could both be the One God? There are two basic answers to this dilemma. One group, the Arians, agreed that the Trinity is illogical as well as impossible, and so they denied the claim that Jesus was equal to God. This group, however, was outvoted in 325 A.D. at the Council of Nicea. The majority opinion, forced to choose between logic or Jesus, chose Jesus. So the question remains— how can any intelligent, logical, clear thinking person accept the belief that 3 could equal 1? Would you wish to give me three dollars for every one that I have, on the basis that three could equal one? If not, why worship such nonsense?

The Christians will respond by saying that they worship three aspects of divinity, not three separate beings. But they also feel that Jesus is separate from God. (After all, Jesus was born from a human mother, he was physical, and he was killed. All of this happened to the supposed son of God, but not to God Himself.) One should ask the Christian if God also died when Jesus died on the cross? If Jesus and God are inseparable, then God must have also died. If so, who resurrected God?

B2. If Jesus had God for a father, then, since God is not a descendant of David, and the Messiah must be a descendant of David, how could Jesus be the Messiah? If you read the first chapter of Matthew, it very carefully shows that Joseph (who was married to Mary, the mother of Jesus) came from King David. Then, in verse 18, it says: *"Now, the birth of Jesus Christ was on this wise: When as his mother Mary was espoused to Joseph, she was found with child of the Holy Ghost. Then Joseph, her husband, being a just man, and not willing to make her a public example, was minded to put her away privately. But while he thought on these things, behold, the angel of the Lord appeared to him in a dream, saying, Joseph, thou son of David, fear not to take unto thee Mary thy wife, for that which is conceived in her is of the Holy Ghost."* Now, one may or may not wish to believe tht God had sex with Mary, but one thing is certain—Joseph was not the father of Jesus, according to Matthew. In fact, Joseph wanted to quietly divorce Mary, for he throught that she committed adultery. (That, too, is an interesting question—if Mary was married to Joseph at the time she became impregnated by God, if she really was impregnated by God, wouldn't that still make Jesus a bastard, for the father of Jesus was not the husband of the mother—?) So the question remains—how could Jesus be the Messiah, which the Christians claim that he is, if his father was not from the descendants of David? God is not a descendant of

David, and yet God was supposedly his father, so how could Jesus be the Messiah? After all, even the Christians agree that the Messiah must be from the family of David.

Some Christians have answered this question in a most unusual fashion—they claim that Mary was from David! Of course, this answer is terrible, because there is no source for that. In addition, Matthew 1 spends 15 verses listing male names only, and the geneology that is found in Luke 3 constantly states, *"the son of," "the son of,"* etc. Furthermore, as everyone who knows the Bible will testify, geneologies always follow the fathers only, which is why Matthew 1 follows the geneology of the fathers only.

Other Christians may answer that since Joseph was, in fact, from David, that is enough to qualify Jesus for Messiah-ship. But that is absurd. In Jewish law, one follows the real father, not the husband, and if the father is not the husband (and the mother is a married woman, as Mary was), then the child is illegitimate.

So how could Jesus be the Messiah?

B3. How could Paul over-rule Jesus? In Matthew 5:17, Jesus said, *"Think not that I am come to destroy the law, or the prophets: I am not come to destroy, but to fulfill. Whosoever therefore shall break one of these least commandments, and shall teach men so, he shall be called the least in the kingdom of heaven; but whosoever that shall do and teach them, the same shall be called great in the kingdom of heaven."* This is in the famous Sermon on the Mount, and if you go through the entire sermon, you will see that Jesus never advocated disobedience of Torah law.

Thus, if you look up Matthew 12:1-5, when Jesus was accused of violating the Sabbath, Jesus did not say that one no longer must observe the Sabbath. Instead, he tried to show that his behavior was consistent with Torah law. From the New Testament, you will not find Jesus rejecting the observance of the laws of the Torah. In John 9, or Matthew 15, for example, Jesus is accused of disobeying Rabbinic law, but not Torah law.

Paul, however, changed all of this. In Acts 13:46, Paul admits that he failed to convince the Jews that Jesus was divine. He therefore went to the Gentiles. However, as Acts 15:1 points out, he was about to meet failure again, for many felt that all believers in Jesus must be circumcised, and apparently the Gentiles opposed that strongly. To solve this dilemma, Paul, in Acts 15, made a most dramatic change. From then on, Gentiles no longer needed to obey Torah law, nor did they need to be circumcised. Thus, Paul said that believers in Jesus need not obey Torah law, and Jesus said you must obey Torah law! And the Christians follow Paul, not Jesus! Isn't that ridiculous?

The Christians have various answers to this question. Be aware, however, that Messianic Jews themselves agree that Jews who believe in Jesus must still observe Torah law, and only the Gentiles were given a dispensation from Torah law by Paul. This does not answer the question, but it points out that even some of the Christians are bothered by this question to such an extent that they keep kosher, observe the Shabbat, etc.

One answer that you might hear from the Christians is that Jesus was referring, in Matthew 5, to the Ten Commandments only. That is openly refuted by Matthew 5:38 and 5:43, for neither of those laws are in the Ten Commandments.[11]

Another answer given by the Christians is that total belief in Jesus is the same thing as observing the laws of the Torah. Belief in Jesus is the fulfillment of the law, and Jesus said, in Matthew 5:17, that he came to fulfill the law. However, this argument cannot explain the problem of Acts 15—if belief in Jesus is enough, and that is what Jesus meant, then what was the problem all about in Acts 15? Obviously, the apostles themselves understood from Jesus that everyone must obey Torah law even after the death of Jesus. Furthermore, Acts 15 gives special dispensation to Gentiles only. What gives Jewish believers in Jesus the right to disobey Torah law?

11. The Ten Commandments are located in Exodus 20.

There is another answer that one could offer, but it creates even more problems. One could say that in Matthew 5:32, 39, and 44, Jesus is openly disagreeing with Torah law; and so, since Jesus said that Torah law no longer need be observed, we do not have to observe it. This, however, is unsatisfactory, because if it were true, again, what was the commotion all about in Acts 15? In addition, Matthew 5:19 makes no sense. Jesus says that whosoever shall break the least of the commandments shall be called the least in the kingdom of heaven; and the law Jesus is referring to seems to be the Torah law, for he said, *"Think not that I am come to destroy the law, or the prophets."* "The law" refers to a specific legal system, of which the people in Israel in the time of Jesus had only one, and that was Torah law. "The Prophets" refers to the Old Testament, and everyone agrees that nowhere in the Old Testament do you find that the prophets disobeyed Torah law, or advocated disobedience to it. The last prophet of the Old Testament, in the last chapter of the Old Testament (in the King James Bible's sequence), says, *"Remember ye the law of Moses* (note: "the law"—just as in Matthew 5:17) *my servant, which I commanded unto him in Horeb for all Israel, with the statutes and judgements"* (Malachi 4:4). Thus, how could Jesus say that one must obey the law of Moses and the prophets, and then say that we do not have to obey them? If Jesus, in fact, said that we must obey Mosaic law, how could Paul disagree with Jesus, the supposed son of God?

This question is a rather complicated one, but a most revealing one, for it shows that Christianity is a religion of convenience, not of truth.

B4. If the concept of the original sin is correct, why did the entire Bible (Old Testament) ignore it? The Christians feel that because of Adam's sin, man lost the ability to achieve eternal bliss on his own and he therefore needs Jesus to help him. Man is also condemned to sin unless Jesus again helps him out. Man is born a sinner, and will die a sinner, unless he accepts Jesus, who died in order to atone for that original sin.

The problem, however, is that the Torah never seems to feel that man is condemned to sin, and on the contrary, states the opposite. Earlier, on pages 44 and 45, various verses from Deuteronomy were quoted that showed that the Torah feels that the laws of the Torah are not too difficult, they are not far off or too hard to obey. On the contrary, you can do them, and you will be blessed for doing so. Choose life, says God—it is in your hands, it is up to you; you do not need anyone else, nor can anyone else help you. This is the message of Deut. 28 and 30. If you look throughout the book of Joshua, Judges, Samuel, etc., you will look in vain for anything which indicates that man is condemned to sin. On the contrary, in 1 Samuel 15, Saul was commanded to destroy all that belonged to Amalek, and Saul, meaning well, spared the best of the sheep for an offering to God. Samuel the prophet then told Saul, *"Hath the Lord as great delight in burn offerings and sacrifices, as in obeying the voice of the Lord? Behold, to obey is better than sacrifice, and to hearken than the fat of rams."* Samuel is clearly saying that Saul should have obeyed, that God wants him to obey, that obedience is within the potential of man—which is really the exact opposite of the doctrine of the original sin. Why then does the Bible seem to state the opposite of the Christian concept of the original sin?

B5. If it is wrong to resist evil, would it be wrong to shoot a potential murderer or rapist? Would you shoot someone who is about to rape your mother or wife? Jesus said, in Matthew 5:39, *"That ye resist not evil, but whosoever shall smite thee on thy right cheek, turn to him the other also."* Many Christians have told me that they would, in fact, not have killed Hitler in the early 1940's because of this principle of Jesus. Thus, in effect, those Christians are tolerating evil, which itself is evil. To say that one should not prevent a murder, by force, if necessary, is to condone murder itself. Furthermore, a good Christian would agree that if a burglar came and was caught robbing you of your jewelry, that you should not punish him or judge him, since that would be a violation of the above verse as well as the mandate of Matthew 7:1—*"Judge not, that ye be not judged."* So if you catch a burglar with your jewelry, give him the keys to your car as well. This, of course, would only make burglary very, very tempting.

The truth is, of course, that most Christians disobey this law because they realize the stupidity of it. Leo Tolstoy, however, in his later years, made it his mission in life to try to convince Christians to obey that law. His campaign itself shows that every one else disobeyed it. (Read *The Widsom of Tolstoy* published by the Philosophical Library.) Not only that, but the Church itself did not obey that law, for Pope Urban II himself initiated the Crusades to rid Palestine from the infidels who were attacking the Christians who were going on their pilgrimages to Palestine (in addition to the Church's other evils which it perpetrated, which we have already discussed).

Some Christians may try to explain this law of Jesus to mean that if someone is in need, then be nice to him. Thus, if someone had to beat you up in order to express and release his hostilities, then turn your other cheek to him also. This, of course, is very forced, not at all what the words seem to indicate, and in addition, it makes the entire verse become unnecessary. That verse is in Matthew 5:39, and later on, in verse 42, Jesus says, *"Give to him that asketh thee, and from him that would borrow of thee, turn not thou away."* Thus, verse 42 seems to discuss someone in need, and since that seems to be the first mention of a person in need, it seems rather clear that the previous verse refers to one who is "evil," not one in need. Furthermore, if indeed verse 39 were to be discussing someone in need, and it is saying that one should let himself be beaten for another's needs, then verse 42 is totally unnecessary, for if you must be beaten, surely one does not have to continue and add that you should loan money to one in need also. If you have to give your body itself, surely you must give your cash as well, so why mention it? It makes more sense to say that verse 39 discussed the resistance to evil, and verse 42 discussed taking care of a person in need; two separate topics, and both need to be discussed. Thus, the question remains—if we do not resist evil, isn't that the same thing as tolerating, and in effect, promoting evil? Isn't Jesus advocating the perpetration of evil?

B6. Isn't the Christian opposition to sex psychologically harmful? In 1 Corinthians 7:1-9, Paul says *"It is good for a man not to touch a woman. Nevertheless, to avoid fornication, let every man have his own wife, and let every woman have her own husband. . .Defraud ye not one the other, except it be with consent for a time. . .and come together again, that Satan tempt you not for you incontinency. But I speak this by permission, and not of commandment. For I would that all men were even as myself. . .I therefore say to the unmarried and widows, It is good for them if they abide even as I. But if they cannot contain, let them marry, for it is better to marry than to burn."* These are powerful words—it is better to marry than to burn. If that doesn't make a Christian feel guilty every time he or she has sexual relations, even with their spouse, nothing will. This Christian attitude goes completely against the basic human sexual drives of man. It does not try to control or guide the sex drive, but rather, it tries to eliminate it altogether. Paul urges that unmarried people never have sex, and those who are married are to try to limit it as much as they both consent to (verse 5). Christianity thus goes against the nature of man. It urges man to repress and destroy one of man's strongest drives, and so, Christianity will inevitably make all Christians reach a stage of neurosis, at least, if not worse. So why become a Christian—won't it make you a psychological mess? If you don't have sex, you will go crazy, and if you do, you will feel quilty—does that sound like something any sane person would want to join?[12]

12. It should be noted that the Jewish attitude toward sex is virtually the opposite of the Christian view. The Torah teaches that it is a Biblical obligation to have relations with one's wife, and the Kabbalists have even gone so far as to use the sexual act as the prototype of God-human relationships. For a good summary of the difference in view between the Christian view of sex and the Jewish one, read the book by David Feldman called *Birth Control in Jewish Law* (or, in paperback, *Marital Relations, Contraception and Abortion in Jewish Law*), chapter two.

B7. Isn't Christianity psychologically harmful, because of the way it limits man? Christianity is based on a major principle, and that is that man is condemned to sin, and will burn in hell forever, unless he is saved from hell by accepting Jesus in his heart. Thus, as we pointed out before in question B4, Christianity rests on the assertion that man is weak, he is a sinner, and he can never achieve saintliness through action. This doctrine will necessarily make man feel weak, it will make a person feel incompetent, insecure, and worst of all, always guilty. This is psychologically harmful, for people thrive the most when they feel positive about themselves. The Jewish teachings have always been that man can overcome evil, man could be holy and wonderful, and that man is precious. In fact, the Talmud states that the reason why God created only one individual human at first is in order to teach man how unique and precious he is, so that it is perfectly justified to feel that the entire creation was justified for any one human being.[13] The Jew therefore walks around being aware of the difficulties, aware of his weaknesses, but positive and confident. The Christian walks around thanking Jesus for sparing him from hell. Isn't that unhealthy?

B8. If it is impossible to avoid being cursed by God, without Jesus, the why did God wish to curse us? This, of course, is a very vague question—let me elaborate. In Galatians 3, and elsewhere in the New Testament, Paul teaches that one cannot achieve eternal bliss by doing good deeds. Paul teaches that everyone is bound to do evil deeds, or at least disobey God's commands to do good deeds, and God has cursed everyone who disobeys a law of the Torah (Deuteronomy 27:26—*"Cursed be he that confirmeth not all the words of this law to do them."*). From Isaiah 64:6 and Ecclesiastes 7:20 Paul deduced that man is condemned to sin (see earlier page 42 for a full discussion on this.) Thus, since everyone must sin, and any sin invokes the curse of God, we

13. Sanhedrin 37a.

are all cursed. We have already demonstrated the gross error in the Christian interpretation of the verses of Isaiah and Ecclesiastes, but the real question is—what did the Christian think of God? Think about it: after the sin of Adam, when man supposedly was condemned to sin, God gave the entire Torah to the Jewish people at Mount Sinai. Now, if God felt that they were all condemned to sin, and that every sinner would be cursed, then the only way to understand God is to say that He is a sadist of the worst sort. If the Christians are correct, then God wanted to curse everyone, because He gave them commands which He knew they could not always obey, and He had a curse waiting for anyone who sinned. The Jews have always looked at God as a Father who loves His people. The Christians feel that He was a sadist, who then changed His mind, and decided to kill himself in order to grant atonement for the world (or is it to atone for his sadism?). Does the Christian approach makes sense? Is God a sadist?

(The real explanation of that verse in Deuteronomy is really what the words say, even according to the translation of the New Testament, if you read it carefully.[14] God is not saying that if you disobey the law, you will be cursed, but rather, one who does not uphold the law (see the original Hebrew) shall be cursed. He who does not support the observance of the law shall be cursed; as the New Testament says it—one who does not confirm the law will be cursed. It does not say, "Cursed be he that does not obey the law," but rather, "he who does not maintain, uphold the law."[15] The Christians, however, did not

14. You should note that Paul has a different translation, in Galatians 3:10, than the way the King James Bible has it in Deuteronomy. The King James translates Deut. 27:26 as, *Cursed be he that confirmeth not all of the words of this law to do them.";* Paul quoted it like this: "Cursed is every one that continueth not in all things which are written in the book of the law to do them." Notice the difference: Deuteronomy says "confirms"; Paul says "continues." Paul reads it to mean that one must continually obey everything that is in the book of the law, or be cursed.

15. A proof that the translation of Paul is incorrect is that Deuteronomy 27:15-25 would really be unnecessary if Paul were correct. If a person is cursed if he disobeys any law, then why mention, for example, that he is cursed for making an idol (verse 15)? That law was already mentioned in Exodus 20:4 and is included in Deut. 27:26, so why mention it again in verse 15?

want to observe Jewish law, because then nobody would want to accept Christianity (see Acts 13 through 15), and so they had to devise a theory whereby the observance of the law itself became unimportant.)

Furthermore, according to the Christians, are all of those humans who died before the birth of Jesus cursed forever? From Sinai until Jesus was around 1200 years—are all those people cursed forever? Is God a sadist?

B9. Could you give me one really solid proof that Jesus is the real Messiah? Without using any circumstantial evidence at all, could you prove that Jesus is the Messiah? You see, the Christians do not have a single solid *proof*—they have only circumstantial evidence of the weakest sort. They will show you verses that could refer to Jesus, but could just as well refer to many other people. They will show you verses that do not refer to Jesus at all, but they twist them to such an extent that they can then claim that it does refer to Jesus. If you go through all of the "proofs" in the first section, you will see that they are all vague, and, in addition, if you read about the life of Jesus, you will see that there is hardly any evidence whatsoever about the life of Jesus except that which is written in the New Testament. Thus, since almost all, if not all, of the Christian "proofs" depend on the historical accuracy of the New Testament, and since the historical accuracy of the New Testament cannot be verified by external sources, the entire Christian "proof" rests upon circular reasoning. Here is the essence of all Christian proofs:

The Old Testament says the following about the Messiah: "XXXXXXXXXXXXXXXXXXXXXXXXXXXX"; The New Testament says that Jesus fulfilled "XXXXXXXX-XXXXXXXXXX"; Therefore, Jesus is the Messiah.

The problem is that one has no way of knowing if Jesus actually did fulfill the prophecy, except by trusting the Christian historians, which means that, ultimately, the Christian proof is simply: Jesus is the Messiah because I say so. This, of course, is no proof at all. The Christian proof is either circumstantial, or based on a history which only the Christians possess.

In short, if a Christian missionary approaches you, ask him or her if they could supply a proof that would resemble a scientist's proof. First describe the type of proof which a scientist would accept and then ask them if they could supply something similar to that. They, of course, will probably say that they could, but after the first sloppy "proof," ask them again to supply only scientific proof, and keep on asking for that. I assure you—it cannot be done—they have no *proof*.

B11. If only faith is important, then why do works? Paul, in Galatians 3, goes into a long tirade pointing out that faith is the only crucial matter, for *"the just shall live by faith"* (verse 11) and *"no man is justified by the law in the sight of God."* Thus, faith in Jesus will create life, not works, for works will only invoke the curse of God (see earlier question B8). As Paul says it, in verse 26, *"for you are all children of God by faith in Christ Jesus."* However, in Galatians 5, Paul explains that *"For in Jesus neither circumcision availeth any thing, nor uncircumcision, but faith which worketh by love"* (verse 6). *"For all of the law is fulfilled in one word: Thou shalt love thy neighbor as thyself"* (verse 14). And in verse 19, Paul specifies those *acts* which a Christian must not do. They include the following: "adultery, fornication, idolatry, witchcraft, hatred, strife, heresies, murder, drunkeness," etc. Thus, Paul is saying that there are certain *actions* which must be avoided. Why? If faith is all that is critical, why mention acts? If man is condemned to sin, then why command him not to sin? How are these commands of Paul any different from the laws of the Torah? They are all based on the laws of the Torah, and Paul said that man cannot help but disobey them, so why did he turn right around and command them again? Obviously, because Paul felt that acts, too, are important—but, if so, why is faith so important, why is it the only critical element? Furthermore, in Acts 16, Paul had more rules—*"abstain from things strangles, and from blood."* How can this be explained?

If works lead to a curse, and if man must sin, why did Paul contradict himself? The truth is, most probably, that Paul knew that works are possible to command, and that works are important, but Paul had to somehow squeeze in the doctrine that faith in Jesus is paramount. His argument was good enough for the ignorant, unsophisticated pagans in his neighborhood, but is it good enough for anyone who could think?

B12. If man is condemned to sin, then how can man be responsible for his crimes? As we have mentioned many times already, Christianity rests on the theory that man is condemned, after the sin of Adam, to sin. Man must sin. If so, is man ever guilty? To the Christian, man is born defective, he is born with a defective soul, and so, how is such a person any different from someone born with a severe mental disability? A retarded person who kills is not evil, so how can a person, born to sin, be considered evil? If you say, indeed, he is not evil, then in that case one must be consistent and never punish anyone again, because their crimes are not their fault, but rather, Adam's fault. Hitler was therefore not evil, the Romans were not evil when they fed Christians to the lions, or when they slaughtered the Jews all those years. Nobody is evil, and therefore we must not punish anyone. Should anyone rape your wife or daughter, the Christian will say that he could not be considered evil. This is one consequence of their doctrine. The other consequence is that man must end up feeling less responsible for his actions. Not only will he feel that he is not guilty, but also, not responsible. The result will be that man will become less careful and cautious, for only if one is responsible will he be careful. A child feels no deep sense of responsibility, and is therefore not careful with whatever he may play with or touch. The greater the sense of responsibility, the greater the caution. Since Christianity eliminates all deep sense of responsibility, it necessarily also removes all deep concern and sense of caution. Does this makes sense? Would you like to live next door to such a person, who feels irresponsible for his actions? (True, many Christians act responsibly, but that is because they ignore this message of Paul, or because they intuitively know that it is absurd.) So the questions remain—if Christianity is correct, is man ever guilty? Is man ever responsible? Doesn't Christianity eliminate all deep feelings of responsibility for our actions?

B13. How can one reconcile the Christian image of Jesus with the way Jesus is portrayed in the New Testament? As you will see, the New Testament itself points out the flaws in Jesus' character, and it shows him to be a rather spiteful, nasty fellow. This is surely not the way a Messiah, a producer of peace and love, is supposed to be. If, for example, you look at Matthew 10:34-37, you will find the following: *"Think not that I am come to send peace on earth; I came not to send peace, but a sword. For I am come to set a man at variance against his father, and the daughter against her mother. . .he that loveth father or mother more than me is not worthy of me; and he that loveth son or daughter more than me is not worthy of me."* This picture of Jesus is far different from the picture of the Messiah that is painted in Isaiah 11, where Isaiah says that the Messiah will bring so much peace that the lion will even be at peace with the calf, and the wolf will be at peace with the lamb. Jesus comes in the name of the sword, whereas the real Messiah is to come in the name of peace! Look at Matthrew 21:17-19: *"And he left them. . .in the morning, as he returned into the city, he hungered. And when he saw a fig tree in the way, he came to it, and found nothing thereon* (in Mark 12:13, the same story is told, and the reason is given— there were no figs on the tree because it wasn't the season for figs to grow), *but leaves only, and said unto it, Let no fruit grow on thee henceforward for ever. And presently the fig tree withered away."* This story is truly remarkable. Somehow the editors seems to have slipped when it was allowed to be published in the New Testament! Jesus was so upset when he discovered that the fig tree had no figs, even though it was out of season, that he destroyed the tree! Why was he so vindictive to a tree, which has no control over itself, and why did he destroy, when he could just as well have created figs to grow instead? Is that the way a Messiah, a man of peace and harmony, is supposed to act? If Jesus did those kind of things, why should anyone consider him to be a Messiah? See Luke 14:26, where Jesus, the supposed man of peace, says, *"If any man come to me, and hate not his father, and mother, and wife, and children, and brethren, and sisters, yea, and his own life also, he cannot be my disciple."* Imagine what it takes to be a true Christian; one must hate everyone, even himself! The Messiah of the Old Testament will bring love, and Jesus teaches hate, and yet some people can still think that Jesus is the Messiah! Perhaps one might be tempted to say that Jesus may indeed have been a hateful, nasty fellow, but his disciples were lovely people, but even that is not true. Paul, himself, in 1 Corinthians 9:18-23, proudly states that he was a full fledged hypocrite and liar, for he admitted that, *"When I preach the gospel. . .unto the Jews I became as a Jew, that I might gain the Jews; to them that are under the law, as under the law, that I might gain them that are under the law. To them that are without law, as without law, that I might gain them that are without law. To the weak became I as weak, that I might gain the weak; I am made all things to all men, that I might by all means save some."* Paul is unashamedly saying that he lied, and deceived, so that he might succeed in his goal. Would you buy a used car from Paul, after you heard this?

Thus, the New Testament itself seems to indicate that Jesus and Paul were not the lovely people that they are claimed to be. They are vindictive, hate-breeding liars, rather than Messianic producers of peace, gentleness, unity and brotherhood among men.

The Christians may respond to these comments by saying that one should not intrepret these passages literally. It means something else, and the true Christian spirit and insight will shed the true meaning of these verses. This seems a bit far-fetched, but moreso, it exposes a far deeper problem. If only the Christian has the true interpretation of the Christian Bible, and if the Jew is to follow and accept the Christian interpretation of the Christian Bible, then, to be consistent, the Jew should be able to similarly demand that only the Jew is qualified to interpret the Jewish Bible. Thus, since all of the Jewish scholars felt that Jesus did not fit the description of the Jewish Bible's version of the Messiah, and since all of the verses which the Christians attribute to Jesus are explained differently by Jewish scholars, then, to be consistent, we should follow the Jewish interpretation of the Jewish Bible, and follow the Christian interpretation of the Christian Bible. It is extremely arrogant for the non-Jew to tell the Jew how to read the Jewish Bible, just as it would be extremely arrogant for the Jew to tell the Hindu how to interpret his holy texts. Thus, if the New Testament is to be read literally, then Jesus and Paul were rather nasty and deceitful people. If it is to be interpreted, and interpreted by the Christians only, then in that case, the Old Testament should be interpreted by the Jews, only. Either way you look at it, Jesus is not the Messiah, for the Jewish interpretation excluded Jesus 2,000 years ago.

B14. How could James contradict Paul? Somehow, the New Testament includes two epistles that are absolutely contradictory to each other. The epistle of Paul to the Galatians is the opposite of the epistle of James! Paul, in Galatians 3, says *"that no man is justified by the law in the sight of God. . .for the just shall live by faith. . .Christ hath redeemed us from the curse of the law. . .the law was our schoolmaster to bring us unto Christ, that we might be justified by faith. But after faith is come, we are no longer under a schoolmaster."* Thus, Paul clearly feels that the primary focus should be on faith, and the law is merely a curse, an ex-schoolmaster. James, however, in James chapter 2, has an entirely different picture. He says, *"What doth it profit, my brethren, though a man say he hath faith, and hath not works? can faith save him?. . .faith, if it hath not works, is dead, being alone. . .for as the body without the spirit is dead, so faith without works is dead also."* The question that faces us is quite clear: here are two canonized parts of the New

Testament, and they are absolutely contradictory! How can this be explained? Paul disagreed with Jesus and James. Which is the correct understanding of Christian dogma?

B15. How could Jesus accuse God? In Matthew 27:46, it states that while Jesus was being crucified, he cried out with a loud voice and said, *"My God, my God, why hast Thou forsaken me?"* Who was Jesus talking to? The Christians claim that Jesus and the Father are really one, so is Jesus crying out to himself? Is Jesus accusing himself of forsaking himself? The true explanation is probably that the author of Matthew did not believe in the Trinity at all. If so, why should a Christian believe in it, let alone a Jew?

B16. Is it true that your god wore diapers? The Christians believe that Jesus was born and raised as a regular human. He therefore went to the bathroom when he grew up, and made in his diapers when he was young. Of course, while it may be a personal objection, I have difficulty understanding how anyone could worship, as God, someone who made in his diapers.

SECTION THREE

The following is a slightly edited series of letters between a Messianic Jew and myself. (A Messianic Jew is a Jew who accepts Judaism and who may in fact observe all 613 commandments, but who also accepts Jesus as his Messiah, as well as the New Testament. A Jew for Jesus, whom Messianic Jews dislike strongly, is really a Christian in all but name. The Messianic Jew is therefore more of a danger to the innocent Jew.) For the sake of privacy, I will call him "X."

NOTE: DISCUSSIONS WITH CHRISTIAN MISSIONARIES ARE USUALLY TEDIOUS AFFAIRS; THE FOLLOWING IS NO EXCEPTION. IF YOU WISH TO UNDERGO SUCH AN EXPERIENCE, CONTINUE READING. OTHERWISE, CONSIDER THIS SECTION TO BE OPTIONAL READING.

I met "X" somewhere and we had a discussion, after which I asked him to please write me, which he did. I had asked him if he would have killed Hitler in 1942, had he had the opportunity—many true Christians would not, based on Matthew 5:39 and other verses—and I find this a good place to begin a

95

discussion with a Jew. As usual, the question touched a nerve, and so, let us begin, but let me first advise you to try to *use the footnotes on this section as much as you can—they will serve to let you really understand the subtleties and implications of all of the points being made.*

Dear Samuel,

I write now in response to your queries. You ask, why rescue Hitler in 1942? The specific example you gave was, if Hitler was being swept down the river, why help him?

Many points need to be addressed in a question like this. For example, would the early death of Hitler have stopped the murder of the 11,000,000 people (6,000,000 Jews, 5,000,000 Gentiles) in Nazi concentration camps? If Hitler was so responsible, why were the Nuremburg trials held?[1] Perhaps even greater massacre would have occurred if the Germans would have had a leader who wouldn't sacrifice his armies because of a desire not to retreat. Please read 2 Kings 6:20-23, 2 Chronicles 28:8-15, Proverbs 24:17-18 and 25:21-22, Exodus 23:4-5.[2] These scriptures give a clear message. The enemy in distress such as the example you gave must be helped. When you are called to judgement, and God asks you, why did you not throw your rope to the one you hate, would you

1. This question is really absurd—just because Hitler was evil, it does not mean that everyone else was innocent. Both could be considered evil. The cause for even considering this argument to be valid is because the Christians really do not want to label anyone evil, and the reason for that is because Paul removed responsibility, deep down, from the hearts of the Christians. Reread page 89, question B12.

2. The first thing that a missionary will do is bomb the person with verses. This serves to demonstrate the superior knowledge of the missionary, and it therefore makes the other person more receptive to the ideas of the missionary. It is therefore very important to immediately do what I did in the first letter—slowly analyze each verse quoted, and point out the value or lack of value in those quotes. Usually, the missionaries do not know the Bible well, but rather, are trained by other missionaries to know a select few verses. Once you demonstrate the flaws of those verses, or the inapplicability of those verses to the point of being discussed, the missionary is very much at a loss. My correspondent here, however, did seem to know the Bible fairly well, although without much depth in his understanding, as the entire correspondence will hopefully demonstrate.

Of course, another purpose behind his question is to try to prove that Jesus seemed to fulfill the Old Testament description of the Messiah. (See Section 1.)

respond, I thought he was thirsty so I gave him the river to drink?[3]

Hatred can be a good servant but is a cruel master. Hatred can turn a man from sin or pervert justice.

Psalm 130 is one of my favorites. God is to be feared for his forgiveness. We have all sinned and deserve death,[4] but forgiveness allows life. I worship the God who gives us life.[5]

You ask me for proof that Jesus is the Messiah. I ask you to tell me what you think the Messiah is described to be in the Old Testament. If you believe in a Messiah, what does the Messiah do when he comes? A picture is painted in the Old Testament. What kind of picture do you see?[6]

Your friend,

X

Dear X,

Thanks for your letter.

As far as your comments about not rescuing Hitler, and your quotes, I'm sorry to disagree. Let's look at your quotes:

2 Kings 6:20-23—There it was after the danger was over— they were captives and therefore were no threat.[7]

---

3. Notice two things in this question. The first is that it is a poor question—who would make such an absurd response to God? Second, notice that he does not distinguish between our personal enemy, who may or not be evil, and between one who is really very evil. He calls Hitler an enemy in distress who should be helped. For what purpose? So that he could continue to kill more people? This will be the basis for my response to him—that the Bible differentiates between people who are evil, and those whom you personally dislike.

4. This is the Christian point of view, not the Jewish attitude. See page 81, question B4, and page 85, questions B7 and B8.

5. And yet, as question B8 points out, this same God, to the Christians, condemned everyone to eternal damnation!

6. The usual person has no idea of what the Bible says about the Messiah. The missionary then points out that *he* does know, and then, with permission, proceeds to point out verses such as Isaiah 53 and the other verses of section one.

7. The only way to really understand this dialogue is to go through the trouble of looking up every verse quoted. You will then see how the verses are twisted by the Christians, and you will learn how to respond to any verse which they will quote. If this comment sounds as if I am saying that Christians *always* twist verses, let me qualify that by saying that I am fairly certain that whenever they could twist a verse, or whenever they must twist it to reconcile it with Christianity, they will. Christianity is clearly not at all what the Old Testament teaches, and so they are forced to change the meanings of many verses and passages of the Bible.

2 Chronicles 28:8-15—Here Jews had other Jews as captives and were going to treat them as slaves—verse 11—your *brethren* should not be made slaves by their brethren.

Proverbs 24:17-18—Correct—do not rejoice when the enemy falls, but do make him fall. Unfortunately they must be killed, but do not be happy about it. Thus the Talmud says that when God drowned the Egyptians in the ocean, He did not allow the angels to sing and rejoice.[8]

Proverbs 25:21—Look at all of the verses from verse 8 on. The whole chapter deals with methods of getting along with your neighbors and friends: 9—do not tell secrets, choose your words carefully (11), do not constantly visit your neighbor (17), etc. Verse 21 says that if your neighbor and you get into a fight, give him food rather than a fist so that you become friends again. Furthermore, in the original Hebrew, it says, "the one who hates you," not "your enemy."

Exodus 23:4—Look at Deuteronomy 22:1—there it says, "your brother" twice in verse 1, twice in verse 2, once again in verse 3. Thus the Talmud says that this law applies to the property of Jews only. Thus, Exodus 23:4—your enemy—someone you are having a personal fight with.[9] In that case, since he is a Jew and did nothing wrong, return it to him.

Thus, *none* of your verses teach that one man must aid an *evil* enemy in distress who is likely to harm other people if he is removed from his situation of distress.

You are correct—hatred can be a cruel master, but non-hatred may be the worst of all. Psalm 130—beautiful, I love it too. But why do you *ignore* Numbers 35:31 (see all of chapter 35), Exodus 22:18, 19; Deuteronomy 17:2-7; 25:17-19, etc? We do find that *evil* people are to be punished by man—if God hates evil and tells us to punish them by death, why don't you listen to God? Your verses from Kings and Chronicles never dealt with evil people, as I pointed out, but when God says that they are evil and are to be punished with death, even then

---

8. Megillah 10b.
9. *Your* enemy, not the enemy of God (i.e., an evil person).

do not be happy and rejoiceful. I suggest that you study the entire Bible.

The picture that I see in the Torah about Messiah starts with Isaiah, chapter 2: the whole world will seek the word of God; the word of God will come from Jerusalem; swords will be beaten into plowshares; there will be no more war, nor idolatry.[10]

After Jesus came: the world does not seek the word of God. In fact, the state and religion must be separate in the U.S., Russian, Chinese and other constitutions. The word of God did not come from Jerusalem for 1900 years so far. Swords are still swords. In fact, we now have world wars and nuclear warheads. At least one major religion began after Jesus (Islam).[11]

I believe in a Messiah and from the above it is clear to me that he has not come yet. How in the world can you imagine that he did? And where in the Old Testament is there a mention of a second coming?

Meanwhile, please explain world wars, etc.

With hopes for peace on earth and
goodwill towards all men,
Samuel

Dear Samuel,

Your letter was most interesting and enlightening. You are an expert in logic. The way you reveal the law to me makes me feel under condemnation, perhaps I am condemned, according to your faith. Consider Leviticus 5:27, or 4:2-3; surely God

---

10. You will notice that Christians hardly ever quote this passage and those similar to it, because Jesus has not fulfilled them yet. See page 76, question A7. Notice that the Jew thinks of the Messiah in terms of peace, good will towards all men, and swords beaten into plowshares. The Christian thinks of the Messiah in terms of Isaiah 53—a dead, insulted man, despised by all. The Jew has a beautiful picture before him; the Christian has an ugly one. See page 85, question B7 again—you will see that Christianity makes a person even feel ugly.

11. This question is not coming to show that idolatry still exists, because Islam is not idolatry at all—they worship only one God. However, Isaiah seems to indicate that there will be no more forms of religion except the Jewish one, once the Messiah comes. Thus, since the Moslems do differ from the Jewish and the Christian mode of worship, and it began around 622 A.D., which is after the death of Jesus, it seems to indicate that the Messiah had not come by the seventh century.

judges even if there are not two witnesses.[12] Where is the blood to come from to atone for my sins?[13]

Never did I intend to ignore Numbers 35:31 or any other portion of scriptures. It seems to me that all of chapter 35 speaks of murderers from among the sons of Israel.[14] Tell me where the cities of refuge are.[15] Consider verse 30. It requires two witnesses to put a person to death. As far as I know, no one ever saw Hitler murder anyone.[16] If Hitler should be allowed to die for giving order to murder, then so should King David, see 2 Samuel 11, 2 Samuel 12:1-9. In particular, chapter 11:14, 15, and chapter 12:9.[17] Who is worthy of salvation?

Though I am not living under law (also unable to), neither do you. Leviticus 26:40. Abraham gave his wife into adultery, Genesis 12:10-20; 20:8-18; Moses was a murderer, Exodus 2:11-14, and the incident with David. No Rabbi I know of has ever spoken of the iniquity of our forefathers, but I confess it now that we are descendants of a sinful people.[18] As in Lev.

12. Notice the immediate sensation of guilt (see page 64) that he has, and is trying to make me feel.

13. See page 41.

14. Notice that this does not answer the question. My question was that you see from Numbers 35 that murderers are to be punished—that evil people are to be punished by man—and that seems to be the will of God. His answer is that this applies to Jews only. This is absurd—if God's chosen people are to be punished, surely those who are not "chosen" are also to be punished by man.

15. Notice that quite often, an irrelevant question, such as this one, will be asked by the missionaries. It seems that they will ask anything, under duress.

16. Incredible! Since no one saw Hitler kill, Hitler is not evil! This is absurd—everyone in the 1940's knew that Hitler was the mastermind behind Nazi Germany. Everyone knew about the huge rallies Hitler organized, where he preached Nazi dogma.

17. This is a good question, his first good, solid question. But it is based upon a shallow understanding of that passage, and in the following letters, I will try to force him to see the inadequacy of his understanding, and therefore, show him that this question is not valid.

18. This point is trying to prove that since Lev. 26:40 says that we will confess the sins of our fathers, we are responsible for the sins of our fathers. However, the verse does not say that. It says that after all the grief that the passage discusses will befall the Jewish people, then the people will confess for their fathers sins, of the previous generation, which caused all the grief, and for their own sins. The Jews will say that we sinned, and we sinned in the same manner as our fathers, and so the sin has become entrenched. That is how the Talmud understands this. The key thing, however, is that the verse does not discuss ancient sins at all. And notice the arrogance—he is going to confess the sins of Israel, on behalf of Israel. He wants to feel guilty, he wants to claim that he comes from sinners, and that he is a sinner. That is an amazing attitude to take for a Jew, but perfectly normal for a Christian.

26:41-42, our uncircumscribed hearts must be humbled so that we make amends for our iniquity, then God will remember the covenant of Abraham, Isaac and Jacob. Note in verse 43 that our iniquity comes about from rejecting the law, but obeying the law does not remove our iniquity.[19] Consider King Ahab, a sinful, idolatrous, ungodly man, yet when he humbled himself before God, evil was not brought upon him, 1 Kings 21:27-29.

I like the way Paul expressed the matter. Romans 3:23-24. For all have sinned and fall short of the glory of God, being justified as a gift by His grace through the redemption, which is in Christ Jesus. Consider Habakkuk 2:4, the righteous will live by his faith.

God has returned to me my faith and I put it in the redemptive power of Jesus.[20]

Now this whole matter of discussing the law the way we are, i.e., concerning Hitler, is absurd. In the book of Titus it says, "Shun foolish controversies and genealogies and strife and disputes about the Law; for they are unprofitable and worthless." Hitler has already been judged. The event has finished. Anything else said is speculation or fantasy.[21] I suggest you bend your efforts in this matter to ending the genocide that occurs today in Asia, Africa, and elsewhere.

Now, Isaiah 2 seems to be speaking of the last days, not the coming of the Messiah, as in verse 2. This speaks of the time after the great battle of Har-Magedon. See Isaiah 34, Joel 3:2, 12, 13. Compare Joel 3:12, 13 with Revelation 14:14-20.

Again I ask you, what will the Messiah be like?

With faith in God's forgiveness,

X

19. This, too, is incredible. The verse explicitly says "Because you rejected my laws and commandments," the earth was or will be destroyed, and yet this missionary claims that this verse does not show that obedience to the law is critical. He simply ignored the words of the verse, and read something else into them. Read them yourself, and judge for yourself.

20. Notice that even where God does something, it is still accredited to Jesus. The Christian has a much closer relationship with Jesus than with God.

21. This is not true at all. If a Christian would not kill Hitler in 1942, would he kill anyone today who is about to kill someone else? If he would not kill someone who was trying to kill millions of people, he surely would not kill someone who was trying to kill only ten or so people, and surely not, if he saw someone trying to kill only one person.

Dear X,

Thanks for your letter.

You asked—where is the blood to atone for your sins?

A) Jesus was not offered on the altar, so it could not be his.

B) Leviticus 18:21 is against human sacrifice, as is the whole Torah, *as you know*, so it cannot be yours or Jesus'.

C) Jonah 3:9, 10—God saw that their deeds changed, not that God saw their blood—see Psalms 51:18-19.

So you do not need blood, you need good deeds and a change of heart. Only pagans need human blood.

X, please don't say that no ever saw Hitler murder—are you honestly telling me that Hitler was NOT the direct cause of 12 million human deaths? Let's be honest.

You asked from 2 Samuel 11 and 12—that whole story needs understanding:

a) See Isaiah 1:15, 17—Your hands are full of blood—and how do you change?—wash yourself, verse 17, seek the welfare of the orphan. Thus, the prophets considers a lack of concern for justice to be like murder itself, even though murder was not committed.[22]

b) 2 Samuel 11:3—Why did David ask who she was? Why not rape her regardless of who she was?

c) 2 Samuel 11:4—Why does the prophet stress that she arose from her state of impurity; i.e., she went to a mikva?[23] The prophet is pointing out that David did *not* sleep with her during her period, which is Biblically forbidden.[24] Why is the prophet pointing this out, if, as you say, he anyway violated the Biblical ban on adultery?

22. In other words, we see that the prophets seemed to exaggerate when they described the sins of men. What to us seems like a minor sin was very major to them.

23. A mikva is a collected pool of rainwater, and nowadays, refers to that building where such a pool is kept, so that women, after their monthly period is over, may immerse themselves in it before resuming marital relations with their husbands. For more information about this, see the pamphlet called "Pardes Rimonim" by Rabbi Dr. Moshe Tendler, as well as another pamphlet called, "A Hedge of Roses" by Rabbi Norman Lamm. These can be purchased at any decent Jewish bookstore.

24. Lev. 18:19.

d) If David committed murder and adultery, as you claim, why the peculiar parable in 2 Samuel 12:1-5? What does the parable have to do with murder or adultery, and why is the rebuke so much milder than Isaiah 1:15, if the crime was so much worse?[25]

e) 2 Samuel 12:24—If David committed adultery, then the son is illegitimate and yet the son of Bas Sheva is the one whom God loves and allows to build the first Temple, and God allows him to be a King of Israel!!?[26] That is extremely unlikely. Study the Talmud for the reasons, but for sure, David did not commit murder or adultery.

I am not living under the laws, you claim, because of Leviticus 26:40; I do not see what that has to do with me or you.[27]

Genesis 12:10-20. Please read it carefully—12:12—*"if you say that you are my wife, they will kill me and let you live (and rape you), so say that you are my sister"* and somehow they won't bother either of us. And see verse 17—God made them full of plagues because of Sarah the *wife* of Abraham. Now, we know from 12:5 that Sarah was his wife, so why repeat it?

---

25. In other words, if you read the first chapter of Isaiah, you will see that he says that the people's hands are full of blood, which implies that they are murderers. However, right after that, Isaiah describes the method of washing the hands from blood—by seeking justice for the fatherless and the widow. Thus, to Isaiah, if one does not take care of the poor and the widow, then one is a murderer, for all practical purposes. Thus, if David did a real act of murder and adultery, which is far worse than not pleading in court for the poor and the widow, then the condemnation should have been much, much worse than "your hands are full of blood." Yet, the condemnation to David seems to be much milder. This implies that the sin of David was not as bad as it seems to be.

26. This question is extremely valid according to the minority opinion in the Talmud which would consider the children of Bathsheba illegitimate even if they were born after Uriah died. However, even according to the majority opinion that feels that Solomon would not be considered illegitimate if he was conceived after Uriah died and even if David's act would be considered adultery, still, it is impossible for such a child to be a king of Israel, elected by God Himself, and to be the one who would build the first Temple. Such a person would have to be born holy, and act holy. Certainly, a child of an adulterer and adulteress would be unacceptable.

27. I find it useful to ask them to explain themselves well, rather than to merely throw verse citations at me. Usually, the question disappears. You will notice that he did not continue along this point in the next letter.

Obviously to say that Abraham was treating her like a wife, and that he wanted to treat her as a wife, so please do not accuse him of treating her like a prostitute.

Genesis 20:2. Abraham called Sarah his sister in Chapter 12, and God intervened and protected him and her, so why not do it again? And God again intervenes. Obviously, Abraham did nothing wrong, and nowhere is he condemned. On the contrary, he becomes wealthy.

Exodus 2:11. Listen, please, Moses killed an Egyptian who was about to kill a Jew. If Moses did an act of cold blooded murder, as you accuse him of, how could God let him be the supreme prophet, deliverer of Israel, the one who talks to God face to face (Deut. 34:10). Obviously, it was not murder.[28]

Habakkuk 2:4. The righteous will live by faith. Paul disagreed, believe it or not, because in Galatians 5:14 he said one must *do*, not just *believe*—we must do actions and avoid other actions (verses 18-21). How do you understand this? And the righteous will live by faith—was he righteous before he had faith?[29] The verse said that the righteous will also have faith, but how do you become righteous? If Hitler had faith, will he also "live"?

Paul feels that God gave us a Torah so that we could be under a curse—Paul accuses God of being an anti-Semite![30]

Maimonides says that the Messiah will be a regular human who will make all Jews and mankind follow God, rebuild the Temple, gather all Jews to Israel, and stop all war and jealousy.[31] Do you know anyone who has done that yet?

Please write,
Samuel

28. In addition, Moses was never condemned for that act. The Bible always lets us know when an act was wrong by specifically pointing out the sin, and so, if no condemnation is mentioned, it indicates that nothing wrong took place. That is the usual pattern. Furthermore, verses such as Numbers 20:12 indicate that the striking of the rock, in the desert, was the only sin of Moses. That is far less severe a crime than murder.

29. See page 88, question B11.

30. See page 85, question B8.

31. Maimonides, Laws of Kings, chapter 11.

Dear Samuel,

You inspire me to think of these matters. There is reason and truth with God. How does one measure truth? The truth of God's word brings life, after all is that not the way God created the world. Now when God gave us the law, it was not dead, it had a spirit which was to guide us in paths of righteousness, but we have taken the law into the realm of darkness and corruption. The spirit of life has left the law. Let me demonstrate.

Please open the new testament to Matthew 5:17. Jesus opens here in 5:17-19 saying that he did not come to abolish or annul the Law, but he did come to fulfill the Law. Now observe verse 20, Jesus tells his disciples that their righteousness must surpass that of the scribes and Pharisees. This must have surprised his disciples. After all, how could they be more righteous than the keepers of the law? Verses 21-48 (in fact chapters 6 and 7 also) answer this question. Consider verses 21-26. The law says, "You shall not commit murder" (Ex. 20:13, Deut. 5:17), but Jesus says that if you have anger with your brother you are guilty. I say that murder starts with anger and hatred in your heart. This is the spirit of the law. Sin starts in our heart, and so should forgiveness and repentance. Now, please read 27-30. The law says, "You shall not commit adultery." However, Jesus says that if you lust for a woman, you have already committed adultery in your heart. 29 and 30 vividly tells us we should discard the lusts in our thoughts. These verses are not to be taken literally. Now consider verses 31-32. The law considered is Deut. 24:1, 3, but examine what Jesus says is the spirit of the law (read Matthew 19:1-12 for more details). Verses 33-37 concern laws of vows and the spirit of such laws. Now consider verses 38-42 in detail. The law says, "an eye for an eye, and a tooth for a tooth" (not to be taken literally); also consider the source (Ex. 21:22-25, Lev. 24:17-21, Deut. 19:21). Each case in the law concerns payment or recompense for one who has wronged another. But what Jesus says is that we should not only accept judgement, but be willing to give more than asked. Read the first part of 39. Do not resist him who is evil, read Jeremiah 21:8-10 and

Jeremiah 38:17-18. Now consider the last part of 39. What is being said is that if you have wronged someone and your judgement is to be slapped, be willing to have your other cheek slapped. 40—if you owe someone your shirt, be willing to give him your coat also, and so on in 41 and 42. Now, what do we do if someone unjustly judges us? Jesus answers this in 43 to 48. The law says that you shall love your neighbor but verses 44-47 gives the spirit of such a law.[32]

Again, to reinforce what Jesus is saying in verse 39, read John 18:19-23. Do I get my car keys and walk back?[33] I know, you don't have them.

Now, turning to the points in your letter.

Concerning the blood to atone for our sins:

A) Consider Deut. 21:1-9. The sacrifice there does not occur on the altar. God chooses where the sacrifice is made (Deut. 12:5). The sacrifice on the altar for Blood Atonement (Lev. 17) concerns only the ox, lamb or goat (Lev. 17:3), not God's son.[34]

B) Consider Lev. 18:21 (or Lev. 20:2-5, Deut. 12:31). These laws concern human sacrifice to the god Molech. Consider the case in 2 Kings 3:27 and 2 Kings 21:6; 16:3; 17:17. These kings spoken of here forced their children to be sacrificed. These men had no mercy. Consider Jesus' sacrifice, he went to the cross by his own choice. Read John 10:11-18 and John 15:13. Jesus was not forced to be a sacrifice. Again read Isaiah 53.

---

32. Notice that he only pointed out that the spirit of the law was not observed properly, according to Jesus. However, my question was—is law necessary? To answer that the spirit of the law is also important is, in reality, to claim that the law is important, too. Thus, the question about law and faith is unanswered.

33. When I first met him, I asked him if he would give me his keys to his car, if I would rob him of his wallet, in order to fulfill Matthew 5:39. Jesus does seem to say that if a person robs you of one thing, then give him another. I therefore asked him if he obeys this law of Jesus.

34. This answer will be thoroughly discussed in the following letters, but the immediate matter of interest is that he claimed that only the ox, lamb or goat can atone, not the son of God. I think he is a bit confused here.

C) Read the book of Jonah more carefully. It is true that when God saw the deeds of Nineveh, He relented (3:9-10), but read 3:4-5. The people first believed in God and their deeds showed this afterwards. (Note that Jonah was dead in the fish for three days and then raised up.) Nineveh was a city of Gentiles and therefore not under the law of blood atonement. God does honor humility (even for someone as evil as King Ahab—1 Kings 21:27-29) but atonement for sin requires blood (Lev. 17:11).[35]

All through the law, men are required to give their own life for sins they have committed. A pagan wants human blood to offer up to false gods, it is done by force, and without mercy. Compare this with the almost offering of Isaac in the test of Abraham. I believe that Gen. 22:8 is a prophecy concerning God providing Jesus as our blood atonement.[36] Jesus is the final blood sacrifice.

Samuel, you ask me to be honest concerning the murderer Hitler. Hitler is dead, he has been judged by God. Why do you still hate Hitler? What does it take for you to give up your hatred? This type of hatred leads to lynch mob mentality. I hate genocide, murder, adultery, idolatry, *sin*. Hatred does not combat sin, but the word of God does! This includes the good news that Jesus Christ died for our sins.[37] Do not lead a life based on feeling, rather lead a life based on the truth of God.

35. Notice that he did not answer the question. The question was that it says that God saw that their actions had changed, and that was enough, so why do we need blood. His answer is—because we do, as it says in Lev. 17:11, even though humility also is honored. He also answers that Gentiles do not need blood for their atonement. If so, why should a non-Jew need Jesus to atone for his sins? Thus, if the people of Nineveh did not need blood, then non-Jews do not need Jesus (but Christians say he is necessary even for non-Jews). If they do need blood for their atonement, then why did the people of Nineveh not need blood, but rather, only a change of deeds?

36. See page 54. Note the fact that Isaac was not killed, while Jesus was. It seems from Genesis 22 that God did *not* want Isaac killed, and yet, the Christians still see Jesus in this story, even though Jesus *was* killed.

37. This entire paragraph does not really make sense, if you analyze it slowly. Obviously, not every hatred leads to a lynch mob, only irrational hatred. Furthermore, if Jesus died for our sins, why hate sin? There is nothing to worry about, for you are supposedly forgiven, and anyway, acts will only lead you to a curse from God (question B8), so why be concerned for sin—you are condemned to it!

This is going to be a long letter; are you up for it?

Now let us consider 2 Samuel 11 and 12. Chapter 11 starts out by setting the stage. It is a time when kings go out to battle, but David stayed at Jerusalem. Nowhere in chapter 11 does David act like a king. Verse 2 describes David watching Bathsheba taking a bath. Again read Matthew 5:27-28. Verse 3 describes the status of Bathsheba. Clearly she is the wife of Uriah the Hittite. Verse 4 describes the lust giving birth to sin. Notice Bathsheba's careful attention to impurity laws (Lev. 15:19-24; 18:19) but complete disregard for adultery laws (Lev. 18:20; 20:10; Deut. 22:22). Read James 1:14, 15. We are not so different from David and Bathsheba in this case. When we yield to temptation we are blinded to righteousness. David and Bathsheba were going through the motions of law abiding people by obeying impurity laws, possibly in an attempt to justify themselves, but they were blinded by lust. Now verse 5, their sin had physically and spiritually conceived. Verses 6-13 describes the gestation of the spiritual sin conception. David first tries to trick Uriah into thinking that Bathsheba's baby is his, in verses 8 and 10. Uriah, being a righteous man, does not lie with his wife, as described in verse 11. I think Uriah knew David had done this great sin. Now verses 12 and 13 describe David's last attempt to cover his tracks. David went to the extent of getting Uriah drunk, and still David's plan does not work. Verses 14-17 describe what sin brings forth; i.e., death. David's diabolical plan is set in 14 and 15. Verse 17 gives us the result of this plan. Verses 18-25 relates the difficulty of Joab communicating the death of Uriah to David. Notice David's cavalier response to the messenger in 25. Verse 26, I believe, describes a ritual mourning, a bit more justification in their own eyes, and 27 describes what really was going on, that is, evil in the sight of the Lord.

Now we look at Chapter 12 at the parable that Nathan gives. This parable (verses 1-4) reveals the spirit of David's sin. Verse 1 introduces two men, one rich (David) and the other poor (Uriah). Verse 2 tells that the rich man had a great many flocks (David already had several wives). Verse 3 tells us that the poor man had nothing except one lamb (Bathsheba). When one has little, little has much value. Verse 4 tells of a traveler coming to the rich man; this traveler is Satan (Job 1:7). The verse continues with the rich man offering up the poor man's lamb to this traveler; i.e., David commits adultery with Bathsheba bringing both into the realm of sin (Satan's realm). Nathan does not even have to include the fact that the rich man also kills the poor man in the parable, as shown in verse 5. David says that this man is a son of death, the same term used in 1 Samuel 26:16; 20:31; in each case, one who should die. David is still blind to his sins in telling Nathan that the rich must make restitution for the lamb (Ex. 22:1). How true this law is but how far David is off the mark in seeing who this rich man is. Finally, Nathan must bluntly reveal to David his sin. Verse 9 clearly states that David committed a sin. Verses 10, 11, 12 starts to reveal the events in store for David. David understands finally and repents. Notice David's confession is immediately followed by the Lord causing his sins to pass away. But, still, the child of this sinful union must die, the sword never departed from David's house, and Absalom raped his concubines. The fact that David has another child by Bathsheba (Solomon) and that God loves this son is not surprising, since God is loving and forgiving (John 3:16).[38] We might examine the geneology of David briefly. Consider Perez the son of Judah and Tamar (Lev. 18:15; 20:12); he is born of a sinful relationship but God forgave; or Ruth, the Moabitess

---

38. It is important to note that I asked four specific questions, and this long discussion only attempts to answer two of them. He tries to answer why the prophet pointed out that she was ritually impure—in order to point out the hypocrisy. (Does that seem to be the impression you had when you read the passage?) He also answers the question of Solomon's eligibility to be king of Israel, and says that it is because God is forgiving. You might ask—if so, why did God kill that baby that resulted from the first union of David and Bathsheba, if He is so forgiving? One sentence describes that the child from the sinful union must die, and the next says that God is all forgiving. One sentence says that the sword must never depart from the house of David, and the next says that God is loving. Does this makes sense?

(Deut. 23:3).[39] It does not surprise me that God can bring righteousness to people like this. Jesus was in the line of these people.

Tell me—if the Talmud says that David did not commit murder and adultery, just what did David do?

Well, that finishes page 1 of your letter. Perhaps I'll have time to respond to page 2 soon. One question about page 2; you mentioned Galatians 5:14, 18-21; are you sure you didn't mean James 2:14, 18-21?

Your friend,
X

Dear X,

Thanks again for your letter.

I do not understand your first main point. In Matthew 5:21, 27, 31, etc., it says, "You have heard". . .—from whom, may I ask? As you surely know, it was from God, in the Torah, and there God says follow these commandments, no more and no less (Deut. 12:32), and that is what I want you to do. So what is happening here? Is Jesus disagreeing with God? Jesus seems to almost insult that which we have heard. See verse 5:43-5— God says hate your enemy, but I say love your enemy, and if you love your enemy, your Father will like you—but the *Father* said *hate* your enemy. Something is very unclear, and I am wondering if you could explain it.

Deuteronomy 21:1-9 is not a sacrifice. It is not called a sacrifice; the Talmud never thought it was. Deut. 12:14 says a

---

39. This, too, is a misunderstood part of the Bible, but I did not want to pursue this tangent. If you study Genesis 38 well, you will see that Judah's sons were to marry Tamar, in order to fulfill the Levirate law/custom, and if they did not, Judah should. After a great delay, Tamar seduced Judah so that he would fulfill his duty. Thus, in the end, Judah states, in verse 26, that Tamar "has been more righteous than I." And, in fact, God seemed to agree, for from that sexual intercourse itself came forth the father of King David, and the Messiah himself is to come from that union (See Ruth 4:18-22). Ruth, of course, did no sin whatsoever, and is one of the models of all righteous women. Why he mentioned her is not clear to me. If it is because she was a Moabitess, that should not make a difference, since she converted (and it was permissible for a woman Moabitess to convert, according to the Talmud, apparently because Deut. 23:5 did not apply to the women). According to the Jewish tradition, Ruth converted to Judaism, married Boaz, one of the judges of Israel. This is hardly sinful, and requires no forgiveness.

sacrifice must be in the specific place which God will choose, not wherever you find a corpse; a sacrifice must be slaughtered whereas here the neck is broken; no blood is sprinkled on the altar;[40] and there is no need for a priest (Numbers 3:10). In short, it is not a sacrifice.

Show me *one* place in the Torah—only one—where God commands us to use human blood as an atonement. And no one is allowed to commit suicide, so to say that Jesus went to the cross by his own choice is to accuse him of suicide. Isaiah 53 could refer to the Jews in Auschwitz or the Jewish people on the whole. Give me one clear *proof* that human sacrifice is allowed. Keep in mind that never in Jewish history were humans ever offered as sacrifices with the approval of the Jewish court and people. The Torah calls it paganism and evil.[41]

Jonah 3:4-5—yes, they believed in God, but what did God see in them that changed things? Did it say that God saw that they believed? Why didn't it say that? I think that you did not answer this point well.

Genesis22:8—On the contrary, Isaac knows fully well that God abhors human sacrifice, and *therefore* he asks, "where is the sheep?" If human sacrifice were Godly, what was his question? And what is this story in the Bible telling us—isn't it saying that even though Isaac was willing to be a human sacrifice, God was against it? I think that one would have to twist everything to see a reference for Jesus here, and I hope that you are intellectually honest enough to see that.

I hate what Hitler represents. He represents evil, and one must hate evil. You apparently love evil men but hate their actions, which makes sense only if they were not the cause of their actions. Jews, however, believe that man has free will, and evil is done by evil people. Many Christians say that the Devil made him do it, which eliminates human responsibility, human guilt, and the human need for atonement. The Jewish

40. See Leviticus 1:5; 1:11; 3:2; 3:8; 3:13; 4:6; 4:17; etc.
41. See Deuteronomy 12:31.

hatred of evil has never led to lynch mentality; the Jews never did the type of lynching that the Crusading Christians did during the Crusades.

With David and Bathsheba, you still did not answer the key questions. If David was a murderer and adulterer, how could he father the next King of Israel? Why wasn't *he* killed instead of the newborn baby? Why the gentle parable of Nathan (as compared to Isaiah 2)? Why didn't the parable discuss murder? Why did God allow the woman who committed "adultery" to mother the next king of Israel? Finally, in Jewish law, when one commits adultery, with a particular woman, he may not marry her,[42] so why was David allowed to remain married to her? Even Nathan had no complaints against that. And your answer about why did the prophet go to the trouble of pointing out that she was pure seems forced. If the prophet was trying to point out her hypocrisy, why didn't Nathan say a word to her??

Thus the Talmud says that all of the men in David's army divorced their wives before they went to war, just in case they disappeared and their wives would not know if they could remarry.[43] Thus, it was not adultery, but it still was not proper, since they planned to remarry as soon as the war was over. Hence the parable.

I *meant* Galatians 5:14-21.

However James 2:14-21 stresses the problem—is it faith or works, or both? If works are necessary, Paul in Galatians 3:10 said that that is ridiculous. If faith alone is necessary, Galatians 5 disagrees. So what is it?

Be well,
Samuel

Dear Samuel,

I will try to be more clear in my explanation of Matthew 5. Jesus gives here a series of Old Testament laws, and then describes the spirit of the law. Verse 43 seems to be causing

42. Sotah 27b.
43. Shabbos 56a.

difficulty now. *"You have heard. . .you shall love your neighbor, and hate your enemy."* Do you wish to tell me that I should hate my enemy? Let us turn to the Torah reference[44] for verse 43, Lev. 18:19. The verse starts, *"You shall not take revenge"* (see Deut. 32:35), then *"nor bear any grudge against the sons of your people"* (see Psalm 103:6-9), *"but you shall love your neighbor as yourself, I am the Lord."* Nowhere in the law does it say "hate your enemy." This is what man added, that is what you tell me that I must do. Perhaps you should read Deut. 12:32; 4:2. What you tell me is that I should bear a grudge against one who is not a son of our people, but I say to you, read Deut. 10:18-19; Lev. 19:34; Ezekiel 47:22-23; Deut. 16:19; 1:16-17; Prov. 11:1; 20:10, 23 and many more references to this point. Just because the laws says that we are to "love our neighbors" does not mean that we are to hate those who are not our neighbors.[45] Jesus tells a most interesting parable about this point, see Luke 10:25-37.[46] Now these scripture lay the foundation for verses 44-47 of Matthew 5.

I sense in your letters and talking with you that you have difficulty with the concept of hate. This is easy to understand considering that just one generation ago, 6,000,000 of our Jewish brothers and sisters died at the hands of murderers. I

---

44. This is his Torah reference i.e., what a footnote in his Bible referred him to.

45. This, of course, is a very poor argument. Imagine, for example, if someone asks you to bring home some ice cream, and you, instead, bring home a salami. If, when questioned about your change, you say, "Just because you asked me to bring home ice cream, that does not mean that I could not bring home a salami," you will certainly be considered a fool. When someone says ice cream, they are excluding everything but ice cream. If God says love your neighbors (that is really an incorrect translation, by the way—it means your friend, or one whom you ought to be friendly with), that does seem to exclude everyone else.

46. Even this parable has a remarkable aspect to it. If you read it you will read a story about a nasty priest, and a nasty Levite, and a very kind Samaritan. You might wonder—what is a Samaritan; who are they? Well, look in Ezra, chapter four, and you will read that the people who lived in Samaria were the ones who tried to abolish the rebuilding of the Second Temple! The Samaritans were the enemies of the Jews, and yet Luke could think of no one else besides a Samaritan to use as an example of a good person! Obviously, Luke had received a very poor reception from the Jews, and this again raises the question that was asked on page 69, in question A1.

too have felt hate, anger, frustration about this act of genocide. But as Lev. 19:18 says, you shall not take revenge nor bear any grudge.[47] Examine these scriptures: Ps. 97:10; Prov. 3:7; 8:13; Job 28:28; Prov. 16:6. In every scripture we see a pattern; i.e., the fear, love and reverence of the Lord leads to a hatred of evil. Hatred of evil or any other behavior or person never leads to a relationship with God. Now, as Eccl. 3:8 says, *there is a time to love, and a time to hate.*[48] Read John 15, where he describes the principle of love (also 1 Corinthians 13), and then contrast this with 2 Samuel 13, particularly verses 15 and 16. Now read Prov. 10:12 and 1 Peter 4:8 and James 5:19-20.

Now, concerning Deut. 21:1-9; this concerns expiation of a crime. Notice verse 8; that is a sacrifice for atonement. The reason that no blood is shed from this sacrifice should be obvious to you. If it is not, read Numbers 35:33-34.[49]

This same verse also answers your question of where is one place in the Torah where human blood is required for atonement. You should ask the question, where in the Torah does it say that another human may die for the atonement of our sins? Often times the law requires the sinner's blood for the atonement of his sins. No where in the law is there any provision for human sacrifice other than the condemnation of it, but note how specific the laws are: Lev. 20:2-5; 18:21; Deut. 12:31; 18:10. All of these laws concern the sacrifice of one's own children (offerings). Why are there no laws about human sacrifice in general? Even so, there is no law to exlude what Jesus did! As far as Jesus going to the cross, I suggest that you read the account in Matthew 26:26 to 27:66; Mark 14:43

---

47. Note that revenge takes place after an event took place, yet our discussion revolves around the elimination of Hitler in 1942, which was *before* much of it happened.

48. As you can see, he does not indicate when is the time to hate. The rest of these verses will be dealt with in the next letter.

49. This is answered on page 122—he confused animal with human blood.

to 15:41; Luke 22:39 to 23:49; John 18:1 to 19:30. He did this act at the will of God. His choice was to do the will of God.[50] Concerning the book of Jonah and the rest of the Bible, the principle is that belief leads to action, never action leading to belief. Consider Genesis 15:6; this is a very important point in scripture. Our nature is so sinful that we distort this fundamental truth.[51] We will believe in anything but God.[52] This is a society that worships the creation, not the Creator. God gives us a wonderful book like the Torah. Tell me—do you love God as much as the book He gives? We are like children, that when we receive a gift, we are so engrossed by it that we forget the

50. Notice that this entire paragraph is illogical. He never answered the question about human blood for atonement, although he mentioned it. He points out that the Torah never provides for human sacrifice, and only condemns it, and then he says that there is no law that excludes what Jesus did! I asked about Jesus committing suicide, and his answer was that Jesus was only doing the will of God. If that is true, why did Jesus cry out, while on the cross, in Matthew 27:46, *"My God, my God, why hast Thou forsaken me?"* If he expected to die, and that was the will of God, this cry makes no sense.

51. If you look up Genesis 15:6, it simply says, *"And he* (Abraham) *believed in the Lord, and He counted it to him for righteousness."* As you see, this verse says absolutely nothing about faith leading to action, even though my correspondent quoted it to prove that point. But worse than that is the next sentence of his, which is a typical move. He will accuse you of being so sinful that you cannot see the truth. If you agree with him, you are not sinful; if you disagree, you are, ipso facto, full of sin. Thus, when the missionaries cannot support their arguments with valid verses that support their point, they use psychology. You must be alert for this.

Furthermore, the entire quote is used in isolation from the rest of Genesis. In chapter 17, God commands Abraham to circumcise himself and his children. Now, if faith alone qualifies to make one be considered righteous, as 15:6 is supposed to indicate, why was Abraham commanded to do an action? It therefore seems clear, from this passage as well as the rest of the Torah, that belief is essential, and therefore Abraham is praised for his belief, but that is not all that is essential. Action is also essential, and from Chapter 22, where God tests Abraham's belief by asking him to sacrifice Isaac, it seems that actions speak louder than words. God did not ask Abraham if he would kill his son, were he to be so commanded. Rather, God commanded him to *do* it. If one does the will of God, rather than simply belief, then he is at the highest level, for Abraham had already shown that he had faith, and God *then* went to test his actions.

52. The human mind can do anything. I, a Jew, am urging another Jew to worship only God, and not God and Jesus, and he can tell me that people will believe in anything but God! As if he does believe in God, and God alone!

one who gives the gift. Read Isaiah 64:6, 7; righteous deeds will not help those who don't believe in God.[53]

Concerning the statement, "the devil made me do it" it is something Flip Wilson, the TV comedian says.[54] It is not in the new testament.[55] In fact, our sinful nature is often enough to lead us astray.

You ask, how could David be the father of the next king of Israel, if he was a murderer and adulterer. It is because our God is the God of the second chance. He is a God that forgives. Consider Judah and Tamar and Ruth. If the Talmud feels that Bathsheba was not Uriah's wife, why did the scripture (2 Samuel 11:3) say that she was; and didn't Nathan say that David murdered Uriah with the sword of the sons of Ammon (2 Samuel 12:9)?

You should read the whole book of Galatians and James. The point of Galatians is given in chapter 2, verse 16. Paul's rule here is carried through the rest of the book. The works of the law do not justify us before God; it is the atonement that Jesus has done for us. A man can be justified before God on his death bed, even if his whole life has been evil. Read Matthew 20:1-16 and Ezekiel 18.[56] The principle in James is totally

53. This is true, but it is not the point being discussed. We were discussing doing versus faith, not the relative quality of various acts and motives. Isaiah himself would agree that it would be better to do an act for a poor motive, rather than not to do it at all. My correspondent claims that he has belief, and yet he still disobeys the law. Is that honest belief? If you told someone that you trust his skills as a doctor very much, yet you refuse to use his services, even though he lives in your neighborhood, and his prices are cheap, wouldn't it be reasonable for that doctor to doubt the integrity of your claim?

54. But it also is really the claim of the Christian Church. The Devil does play a major role in Christian thinking, and, in fact, is the counterforce to Jesus. Read 1 Corinthians 5:5 and Ephesians 2:2.

55. See the previous note: it *is* in the New Testament, and Jesus himself indicated that all those who rejected Jesus are sons of the devil—see John 8:44. (Note that the Jews there claimed that Jesus had *a* devil in him i.e., an evil spirit, but Jesus claimed that they were born from *the* devil.)

56. This is incredible. Ezekiel 18 emphatically stresses the need for proper *action*. *"If a man be just, and do that which is lawful and right...* (and then verses 6, 7 and 8 list many evil actions that he did not do)...*he shall surely live, saith the Lord God."* Verse 30: *"Repent, and turn yourselves from all your transgressions, so iniquity shall not be your ruin."* The entire chapter discusses only action, and the need for proper action. This is why it is essential to look up every quote that a missionary tells you to see. Many times you will discover the very opposite of what they are trying to prove.

consistent. Read James 2:21-26. What it says is that faith leads to works.[57] Abraham believed in God and this lead to action. The Ninevites believed in God and this lead to their repentance. Paul says to the church at Galatia: believe God, and you will be justified. James says that faith leads to works. This is a basic principle of the Bible; i.e., that faith leads to works, but works never lead to faith.

In the meantime, could you please tell me what the Messiah will be like, if He hasn't already come.

Sincerely, your friend,

X

Dear X,

Thanks for writing again.

First of all, you should notice that *every* statement that Jesus quoted in Matthew 5 are all from the Torah. You claim that there is one exception—"Hate your enemy." I am sure that you will agree that if every previous quote was from the Torah, this *last* one is probably also from the Torah. Look at Psalms 5-10; *"You hate all doers of evil; destroy speakers of falsehood; God abhors the man of blood and deceit. . .destroy them."* See Psalms 26:5—*"I have hated the congregation of evil doers and will not sit with the wicked."* The Torah always condemns evil and wishes that we be good and reject evil, while at the same time we must try to change evil to good. In fact, there is a famous story in the Talmud, on Berachos 10a, where it quotes Ps. 104:35. The correct translation is, *"let sin be consumed"* (not sinners), and so the Talmud says that we should try to eradicate sin instead of sinners, if possible. Thus, Lev. 18:17—Do not hate your brother in your heart—verbalize your feelings and try to change him. Whenever it says, "Ger," such as in your verses of Deut. 1:16,[58] etc., it means

---

57. So why did Paul eliminate all of the actions commanded by God in the Old Testament, and why does my correspondent feel that he is excused from doing works? Faith leads to works—what works? What are the works that a Christian must do? And how could you command any works at all—isn't man condemned to sin, anyway? Won't he disobey anyway? The Christian picture here is really very confused.

58. In the original Hebrew, the word for stranger is "ger."

one who has accepted the seven Noachide laws (including not to murder, steal, commit adultery, etc.), not a pagan murderer. This is clear from Deut. 7:1-11, and the sources which I will soon quote. We are not allowed to have evil pagans living in our midst, so the stranger (ger) that is referred to in Deut. 1:16 and elsewhere refers to a non-pagan. That is clear. See Lev. 20:23—do not commit incest like the other nations of Canaan, for I abhor *that* and *them*. God abhors evil and so must we (Deut. 28:9). He also accepts repentance, and so must we. I cannot see how you cannot see this. Deut. Chapter 28—if you Jews are good, may you be blessed; if not, you will be cursed (verses 15 on). I ask you, shouldn't it say, if you are not good, then I will love you and forgive you anyway? Is Jesus more forgiving than God? Deut. Chapter 7—destroy those evil nations—7:2—do not love them, do not forgive them, for they are completely evil. Verse 7:16—destroy them or they will destroy you, by being a snare to you. Jesus obviously is violating the very essence of the Torah when he says that we should love evil or love evil doers. Because of that, *you would* rescue Hitler, which you know is pure idiocy. You said that, in 1942, you would still have rescued Hitler. That is evil! I do not understand your other comment. You quoted Ps. 97:10, which says that lovers of God should hate evil, and then you said that hatred of evil will not lead to a relationship with God. Well, then, why did Psalms encourage it? And two verses later, it indicates that the result will be a rejoicing with God. Isn't that a relationship? Proverbs 3:7 proves nothing except that we should not do evil. You quote Prov. 16:6 to prove something which I do not see—why not look at 16:5? Prov. 10:12—true, hatred that is wrong stirs up strife; hatred of evil does not. Otherwise, Prov. 8:13 and 12:8 etc., make no sense. Eccl. 3:8—a time to love, and a time to hate—when is your time to hate? If you would not hate a Hitler, when is your time to hate?

You *ignored* all of my questions about Deut. 21. Please X, answer my questions. In Deut. 21, no priest is needed, the animal is not slaughtered like all sacrifices, it is not offered on the altar, no blood is sprinkled—it is not a sacrifice unless you want to ignore all of these points.

True, all of the laws are against sacrifice of the children. Where is there, however, a law allowing human sacrifice? How are children's blood different from adult blood? Why is there no mention in Jewish history or tradition of any human sacrifice which was approved by the community? I asked you to show me one place in the Torah where human sacrifice can atone, and you did not show me one. Why not?

Tell me, X, do you love Jesus more than God? God says this, and Paul says that, and so you do not keep kosher, yet you ask me if I love the book more than God. At least I obey Him. Why do you violate the Shabbat, laws of keeping kosher, and then say to your brother that he loves the book more than God? I say to you, brother, obey God, then show me your verses, not the other way around.

Again, you did not answer my questions. Why wasn't Bathsheba condemned at all, why was she allowed to mother the beloved king of Israel, why wasn't David killed like all adulterers, why did David ask who she was before he took here, as if it made a difference, why was David allowed by Nathan and God to marry the woman he committed "adultery" with, why did the prophet point out that she was pure? Why? If God is so forgiving, and the God of the second chance, as you say, why did He kill the newborn baby?[59] What did the baby do wrong? Where was God's forgiveness? How does your explanation make sense??

Faith leads to works. Are works *essential?* Yes or no? If yes, why did Paul oppose that idea and say that faith is the crucial element, and faith alone? If no, why mention them? Please answer this.

The Messiah will be a regular human, religious, obedient to God's will, who will lead the world to peace and to God. Jesus did neither. But in this name, Crusaders killed thousands of Jews. In his name, the Inquisitors tortured and killed thou-

59. 2 Samuel 12:15, 18.

sands of Jews. In his name, Jews were falsely accused of drinking babies' blood. In his bloody name lies thousands of innocent Jewish lives.

Please answer my questions,
Samuel

Dear Samuel,

Regarding Matthew 5:43, see Lev. 19:18. Nowhere in that verse does it say hate your enemy. Do you think that your hatred is right in tune with the will of God? If so, you are better than Jonah.[60]

Concerning Deut. 21. Some sacrifices do not need a priest. Some sacrifices can be done without the temple (Ps. 51:17). The reason the animal is killed in the way it is, is explained in Numbers 35:33, therefore the blood is not sprinkled. If you do not call this a sacrifice, what do you call it?

Consider the laws on human sacrifice. A child would not understand the meaning of willingly laying down his life for another. Therefore child sacrifice is strictly forbidden. An adult would understand the meaning of laying down his life for another. If the adult was unwilling, the act would be prohibited under murder laws. Thus, no legal or moral prohibition against an adult laying down his life for another.

I love Jesus equally with God, for Jesus is equal to God.[61] Jesus atones for my sins so that I am worthy to be in the presence of God. Jesus is my justification.

I'm tired of writing to you about 2 Samuel 11, 12. Perhaps you should read it. It might give some interesting commentary on the Talmud.

---

60. It might be a good idea to look at my response to this letter, and to refer to it, point by point. You will see in my response that he ignored all of my questions regarding this point.

61. The Christians claim that a "separate but equal" rule could apply to God. The leaders of the civil rights movement correctly understood that that is really impossible, and, in truth, the Christians do not really mean it, because they pray to Jesus, they live for Jesus, and it is Jesus that they love. Because the Father expects obedience and the Son does not, the Christians have prudently decided to follow the Son. See page 77, question B1.

Faith leads to works in the same way as a fruit tree gives fruit. Works never lead to salvation, it is faith in God. Why don't you see this?

I see that you have found a scapegoat in the Christians. Who taught you this technique, Hitler maybe?

Explain to me Daniel 9:24-27.

Your friend,
who seeks the truth,
X

Dear X, "who seeks the truth."

I enjoy writing to you because you demonstrate a real knowledge of the Bible. I discovered, however, a habit of yours which will only prevent you from finding the truth. Whenever the questions are strong, you do not answer them. So I may end up asking the same questions as before. Again, I ask, please answer them, and then reflect upon your answer—is it good, is it poor, do you really like it?

1) Matthew 5:43—You say that it does not say in Lev. 19:18 to hate your enemy. But I did not bring up that verse, you did! But I mentioned an entire group of verses, which you somehow ignored completely!? In addition, I pointed out that every other quote in Matthew 5 is from the Torah, so this probably is too. Please answer this question, and explain how Jesus could disagree with God.

2) You say that Jonah did not hate, and I am therefore more evil than Jonah. Remember, please, you brought it up first (i.e., Jonah). Let me ask you—didn't Jonah disobey the command of God—wasn't he almost drowned because of it? and why? because Jonah did not want the people of Nineveh to repent—why not? (If you say because he hated them, than I am not worse than him.) (P.S. The Talmud has a different answer.) So how do you understand Jonah—why did he disobey God?

3) Here you have exposed the worst contradiction that I have seen yet. Please explain yourself: you claim that Deut. 21 does not need a priest or temple because of Ps. 51:17. Well, if that is true, then we also do not need a Jesus to die for us—all

we need is a broken and contrite heart. How do you explain this?

4) You say that the blood of Deut. 21 is not sprinkled because of Numbers 35:33. Please note: Numbers 35:33 refers to human blood, doesn't it? Leviticus commands us to sprinkle animal blood. Deut. 21 refer to an animal, and yet no blood is sprinkled. Numbers 35 says do not spill human blood—which brings us back to human sacrifice—where in the Torah does it condone it? Where does it command it? You said that if the Torah forbade child sacrifice, then it implies that adult human sacrifice is permitted. Are you really happy with that? Do you ever see human sacrifice mentioned in a positive way in the Torah? Using your reasoning, in fact, if in Leviticus, it says that our sacrifices must come from the sheep, cow and dove, doesn't that seem to exclude humans such as Jesus?

5) Deut. 21 seems clearly to be something besides a sacrifice, because of the reasons which I gave. It therefore seems to be a ritual designed to make the elders of the cities realize their lack of concern, to make them realize the depth of the tragedy, just like wearing T'fillin[62] is designed to make a person aware of his responsibilities.

6) Do not be insulted, please. When I asked you if you love Jesus more than God, I asked, if you remember, that God said, keep kosher, observe the Shabbat, etc., and Paul said that you do not have to. So again, who do you obey more? God said keep kosher, Christians do not. You are a Jew—will you obey God? If not, aren't you really rejecting Him?

7) Who do you pray to—Jesus or God? The Jew is commanded throughout the Torah to serve God, to pray to God, etc. Who do you pray to?[63]

8) You wrote, "I'm tired of writing to you about 2 Samuel 11; perhaps you should read it." That is an insult, and you

62. The phylacteries are worn on the arm to remind us to dedicate our muscles to the service of God; they are worn on the head to remind us to dedicate our thoughts and creative energies to the service of God, and the two straps that follow the length of our bodies is to remind us to dedicate our bodies in totality towards being a better Jew.

63. In other words, if the Christians really believe in the separate but equal idea, then why do they tend to pray exclusively to Jesus. Is that called equal?

know it. Secondly, why are you tired? You have never answered my questions. Why are you avoiding them, letter after letter? To find truth requires intellectual honesty, and if your answer is inadequate, or non-existent, then that should bother you, and instead you threw an insult at me.

9) You wrote, "Works never lead to salvation, it is faith in God"—so why do works? Why are works essential—why does Paul insist on works also?

10) Christians are not my scapegoat. A scapegoat is an *innocent* person; are you saying that the Crusaders and Inquisitors did nothing wrong?

11) You asked for my explanation of Daniel 9:24-27. Briefly: 9:24—You will have 70 periods of 7 years each to make atonement (to offer sacrifices), from the end of the first Temple until the end of the second Temple (70 year exile plus 420 years for the second Temple).

9:25—Know, that from the time that the word (of God) indicated the rebuilding of Jerusalem until the annointed one will be seven periods of seven years each, and for 62 full periods of seven will it be rebuilt. The annointed one is Cyrus (see Isaiah 45:1). The Christians put the 7 and 62 together even though 9:26 indicates that they are two separate periods. The Christian way is incredible—why not simply say 69 weeks?

9:26—After the 62 seven years periods, the work of the anointed one (the accomplishment of Cyrus) (or, an anointed one, namely a Jewish king) will be destroyed, and the city and sanctuary will be destroyed. Now, the Christian interpretation says that this entire passage refers to Jesus. If so, why wasn't Jerusalem destroyed in 29 A.D.? Aren't the Christians around six 7's off?

So now I ask you—how do you explain Daniel 9:24-27? And I know it's a lot of work, but please answer questions 1, 2, 3, 4, 6, 7, 9, 10, and 11.

Your friend, really, and one
who also seeks the truth,
Samuel

Dear Samuel,

I will now attempt to answer your questions. Please keep a copy of this letter so that I will not be forced to repeat myself again.

1) Matthew 5:43—It says, *"You have heard that it was said, 'You should love your neighbor, and hate your enemy.'"* It does not say, the Torah says. Jesus perceived how Jewish scholars of that time perverted the law. Even now you would have me believe that this is what the Torah teaches. Consider Deut. 4:2. Exodus 23:5 illustrated an element of this concept. Do not return evil upon one who hates you.[64] Matthew 5:44 says that we should pray for those who persecute you. The question to ask is, what do you pray? Pray that the person repents—that is the will of God. See Ezekiel 18:31, 32.[65]

2) Jonah did hate the Ninevites. I will demonstrate this. Jonah lived and prophesied in the time of Jeroboam II and Uziah. See 2 Kings 14:25; 10:32. Hazael, King of Syria, had taken part of the northern kingdom, and Jonah prophesied the return of part of the kingdom. Now, soon after this time, Israel (northern kingdom) fell to Assyria (2 Kings 17). Now, who lived in Nineveh? See 2 Kings 19:36. Nineveh was a city of Gentiles who warred against Israel and Judah. Jonah may have had friends and relatives die at the hands of people from Nineveh, and so Jonah hated those people; they were enemies of Israel. To put it into a modern perspective, it would be as if God told you to go into Nazi Germany and preach repentance. You would probably do the same thing as Jonah, and go in the opposite direction. Nowhere does God get even close to

---

64. Notice that he still does not see the difference between someone whom you hate for personal reasons, and someone who is evil. The Torah says that we ought to love those whom we hate, and we should love those who hate us, but we should hate those who are evil (because they chose to be evil).

65. Indeed, see those verses and the entire chapter which precedes them. I think that he did not read the entire chapter, and instead knew these two verses which were taught to him. Even so, Ezekiel urges us to *"cast away our transgressions"* in verse 31—that means that we should change our behavior, our actions.

disowning Jonah.[66] Jonah did not want Nineveh to repent because he hated them, and because they did, in fact, repent, God later used them to judge Israel. Thus, you are much like Jonah, B.F.; that is, Before Fish. What does the Talmud say? 3) Concerning Ps. 51:17, may I ask you a question? What breaks your heart? What breaks my heart is sin.[67] See the response of Jesus to sin (Luke 19:41-44). Why isn't your heart broken over the crucifixion of Jesus. After all, he committed no sin,[68] but died to take our judgement. The need for atonement has nothing to do with priests or temple. The first example of atonement can be found in Gen. 3. When man sinned, they realized they were uncovered. God had to make new coverings from skin in Gen. 3:23. An animal[69] died to restore the covering from God; i.e., atonement.

4) Numbers 35:33 makes no mention of the kind of blood being shed.[70] Gen. 9:4 reveals that the life of all things is in the blood. Gen. 9:6 speaks of whose blood God requires for the taking of human life. Therefore, Deut. 21, which speaks of murder, would be in violation of Gen. 9:6 and Numbers 35:33 if the heifer's blood is shed.

66. This should raise a question in one's mind. If God did not get close to disowning Jonah, that implies that Jonah was not doing anything wrong, and yet the story seems to say that he flagrantly disobeyed the express command of God Himself—? If God commands a person to do something, and that person hates that something, that normally is irrelevant—if God wills it, so be it. Thus, the explanation so far seems very inadequate.

67. This did not answer the question at all. I asked him about the need for a Jesus, if Psalm 51:17 says that all that one needs is a broken heart, and he avoided the question completely. Instead, he asked me a question that was hypocritical, for he himself admits that he knowingly sins, and has not made efforts to change.

68. See page 72, question A5.

69. Our whole discussion is about the permissibility of using humans (Jesus) for atonement, and he quotes something about animals. You see, when a good answer is not available, the missionaries will simply throw another quote, and unless one calmly and carefully examines every quote, he might be drowned and overpowered by them, even though the quotes do not prove anything at all, such as in this case.

70. That is true, if you look at that verse alone. Read the entire chapter, however, and it should be very clear to anyone that it refers to human blood. Christians do not seem able to read entire chapters at a time. Very often their proofs, as we have seen in Section One, are based on verses taken out of the context of the entire chapter.

Nowhere does the Torah command human sacrifice. The act of laying down your life for another is not a matter of law, but of love. Read chapter 10 of John and understand this principle, and contrast the chapter with Ezek. 34.[71]

The death of Jesus does not include the death penalty for murderers. Other reasons do. Jesus' atoning death reconciles man and God for eternity, not just our physical lives. Jesus at his death took all the sins of mankind onto himself.[72] This means that even a murderer can be reconciled with God before he dies.[73]

6) If Jesus had not died for my sins, I could not be in the presence of God. But not using light switches or driving on Saturday, or eating kosher, would never cover my sins. Your eyes are well tuned to my faults. Is this the only thing wrong with me or does obeying the dietary laws and the Sabbath laws make me perfect? After all, this is the third time that you have mentioned this.

7) The Father, Son and Holy Spirit are the three entities of God. I pray to all three. Often times I pray to Jesus, especially when I remember the work of the cross and how Jesus reconciled me to God.

8) At least you understood my insult. After all, you did not understand my explanation of how Solomon could be King if David and Bathsheba committed adultery. It is clearly a matter of God's grace and forgiveness. This is nothing new, consider Judah and Tamar and Ruth. Our God is the God of the second chance. Jonah 3:1.

9) Please read Matthew 7:15-23. This describes how works relate to a person. The simple example is the kind of tree

---

71. You will notice that Ezekiel 34 has nothing to do with laying down own's life for another. It simply discusses *sharing* own's food and property with another.

72. If this is true, then why did he say, a few paragraphs earlier, that his heart is broken over the crucifixion?—Shouldn't he be happy, because now all of man's sins are forgiven? Shouldn't the death of Jesus be cause for celebration, since it brought redemption to the world?

73. I do not understand how he derived this principle from the previous comments—was Jesus a murderer?

determining the fruit. In the same way, a person's beliefs determines their behavior. You ask, why do works? I ask you, why does a tree bear fruit?

10) Your response to my calling the Christians "scapegoats" reminds me of the way Nazis refer to Jews. Would you kill Christians because of the Crusaders and Inquisitors? Those men were no more followers of Christ than Karl Marx was a follower of the Torah.[74]

11) I agree with what you have to say about Dan. 9:24, but wonder about 25 and 26. Cyrus was a king, but 25 refers to a prince; compare with Daniel 8:11 and Isaiah 9:6. God did use Isaiah, but Isaiah 45:12 says that God commands the host.[75] Read Mark 15:26. The Romans were mocking but little did they know that Jesus became king at his resurrection. Jesus was crucified in 30 A.D. Again read Luke 19:41-44. I admit that I do not totally understand these prophecies, but surely Cyrus was not the Jewish king of this prophecy.

If you have time, would you please consider and explain these scriptures to me: Ps. 22, Micah 5:2, Deut. 18:14-22, Ps. 110.

Your friend,
X

Dear X,

Thank you for answering my questions, as I have answered yours. However, I think your answers are inadequate, for the following reasons:

1) Matthew 5:43—*"You have heard"*—you said that it means that you have heard this from Jewish scholars of the time, as they would try to lead you to believe. If your interpretation is correct, kindly explain this problem: in the same sermon, in the same chapter, in 5:21, it says, *"it was said*

---

74. Notice that the analogy is invalid. Marx openly denied the validity of the Torah, he wanted nothing to do with it. The Crusaders, on the other hand, marched with a cross on their chests, and in the name of Jesus. Doesn't that qualify someone as a follower of Christ?

75. If this does not make sense, do not worry, because it doesn't. But see how they try to drown you in verses, rather than in logic and solid thinking.

by them of old time "; in 5:27—"*said by them of old time*"; and again in 5:33. Now, "old time" means before the time of Jesus—long before his time—and all three quotes are direct quotes from the Old Testament, if I am not mistaken. If so, isn't it a bit difficult to say that 5:43 is a change from the rest of the sermon, as you would explain it? Thus, again, I ask—does Jesus know more than God?

2) You claim that Jonah did not want to preach repentance to the people of Nineveh because he hated them like some Jews hate Nazis. Are you telling me that a prophet of God, a person whom the Creator of the world speaks to, a person who probably is as close and identical to God as is humanly possible—are you telling me that such a person hates those whom God loves? And your comment about B.F.—Before Fish—look in After Fish, in 4:1-3, Jonah is terribly distressed that God did what he knew God would do—this is after the fish. Why is Jonah so upset, why does he want to die? What is the Christian answer to these questions? And again—Jonah 3:10 —God saw their *repentance*, not someone else dying for their sins!

3) Again you did not answer the question. Why did Jesus have to die on the cross if Ps. 51:17 says that all that is needed is a broken and contrite heart?

Furthermore, you say that your heart breaks over sin, and yet you eat non-kosher. Does sin really break your heart, honestly? Your heart is broken over the death of one man, yet you would not kill Hitler in 1942 to save millions of lives. Obviously, you are rather inconsistent. Could you explain yourself, please.

4) My friend, you have something else confused again: Gen. 9:6 and Numbers 35:33 refer to situations where the courts know who the murderer is; Deut. 21 refers to situations where the courts do not know who the murderer is. Simple and straight. And nowhere does it say that we should taken human blood of one person to atone for another. And you did not answer my question from Leviticus, which says we should

offer sheep, cows and doves, which seems to exclude humans. Please answer this.

5) Yes, I mentioned your not keeping kosher several times, and you have ignored it each time. Let's hope this is the last time. Christians do not keep kosher, not do they have to, according to Jewish law. Jews do have to keep kosher. You do not keep kosher—are you a Jew? Is it because Jesus has forgiven you in advance?

6) You admit that you insulted me, yet offered no apology. Is that what Jesus teaches—don't hate your enemy, just insult him? And again, you did not give me direct, specific answers to those questions about 2 Samuel.

7) Matthew 7:15—I'm confused. You write, "a person's beliefs determines their behavior." Well now, Christians believed in Jesus and killed Jews during the Crusades. Christians believed in Jesus and tortured and killed Jews during the Inquisition. And you want more people to believe in Jesus? It is simply not true to say that the Crusaders were not followers and believers in Jesus. It is an absolute lie. And why do works anyway; you will be under the curse if you do (Galatians 3:10)?

8) I did not look up all of your sources, since the beginning of your question is based on a faulty translation: Daniel 9:25 refers to a "nogid"—a prince or ruler; Daniel 8:11 refers to a "Sar Tzavah"—head of the armed forces; Isaiah 9:6 refers to a "Sar"—officer.

9) Ps. 22—I doubt if it refers to Jesus, since 22:8 indicates that he thought and hoped that God would save him, and I have not seen any indication of that in the New Testament.[76] Even Matthew 27:43 says that he trusted in God, but where do you see that he expected to be rescued? On the contrary, had he been rescued, he could not have become the atonement. 22:2— Jesus cries to God and is not heard? If Jesus is God, why can't he hear himself? Micah 5:2 refers to David, from whom the Messiah will come. Deut. 18:15—just as God speaks to me, so

76. See page 32.

He will speak to others; listen to them, provided they do not tell you to violate Jewish law (Deut. 13:1-5). Psalm 110—see the Hebrew: "God said to my master"—who is the master of David? Jewish commentators, who knew Hebrew, said it referred to Abraham.

Your friend,
Samuel

And so the letters continued, neither of us succeeding in convincing the other.[77] By carefully following the discussion, however, you will see the how the Christian mind works. The footnotes on this section were written so that you could easily see what is happening, and so that you might more fully understand what is really taking place below the surface. If you have not been using the footnotes on this section, it would be worthwhile to reread the section again, and follow the footnotes carefully.

---

77. Once a person has accepted Christianity, especially for psychological reasons, it becomes extremely difficult to change their minds without actually deprogramming them. Logic will usually not suffice, as this correspondence hopefully demonstrated. The main concern is to catch the process before it becomes entrenched. If you see yourself or another in the process of investigating the merits of Christianity, that is when the book is especially useful, since the mind is still functioning at that stage.

CONCLUSION

Let us conclude this investigation of Christianity with the realization that it is easy for millions of humans to believe in nonsense; that it is easy for all of us to believe in nonsense; and that we ought to be careful, very careful, to always check our beliefs, our axioms, and our opinions, for it is very easy to be wrong. Let us therefore be open to criticism of our beliefs, let us appreciate anyone who may help us find the truth, and let us honestly search for the truth. Let us love the truth; let us have no preconceived notions of what the truth is; let us be openminded. As the Talmud says, search for the truth, and you will find it. If you search hard enough, you will surely find it.[78]

In addition, it is very important to remember and realize two things. The first is that Christian missionaries are particularly interested in converting Jews; they are more interested in making a few Jews become Christian, rather than making many pagans into Christians. The reason for this is rather simple. Since the concept of the Messiah is a Jewish concept, and it was taught by the Jews, and the Messiah was to redeem and bring peace to the Jews, it therefore creates great frustration for the Christians whenever they reflect upon the fact

78. Megilla 6b.

that the Jews in the time of Jesus and from then afterwards consistently rejected Jesus as the Messiah. If the Jews rejected him, and he came only in the guise as the Messiah for the Jews, then why should anyone else accept him as the Messiah and redeemer of the Jews and the world? The missionaries therefore are trying their best to convert the Jews first, because it means a lot more to the rest of the world when a Jew accepts the Jewish Jesus as the Messiah of the Jews. Historically, the Christians tried everything, including the sword, and it never really worked, because the Jew refused to drop his religion even on pain of death. Because of this, the Jews for Jesus movement arose, (as well as the Hebrew Christian and Messianic Jewish movement), and they tell the Jews to still remain a Jew, to still act as a Jew, and to care for Jews, but to add Jesus to their Jewishness. Once the Jew becomes a Jew for Jesus, however, it does not take long before that person becomes a Christian in all but name. Thus, it should be understood that the Christians are trying to convert Jews in many different and devious ways. This includes sending literature that is written in Yiddish to lonely elderly Yiddish speaking Jews, and then, capitalizing on their loneliness and ignorance or feebleness of mind, to convince them to convert before they die. Millions and millions of dollars are being spent annually to fund this effort.

The second thing to realize is that virtually every Jew that converts to Christianity knew nothing, or next to nothing, about his or her Judaism, before their conversion. The Christians succeed only where ignorance prevails, and so we must realize that the best way to eliminate the conversion of Jewish people to Christianity is to educate the Jew about his Judaism. If you could support any Jewish educational institution that teaches true Judaism, that teaches the student to love each other as well as to love God, and that teaches the student to love the word of God, then you are stopping the Christian menace. Of course, your own home should be an example of the above, for in the home where spirituality is absent, and Judaism is simply a ritualized game, the children will be easy targets for Christian missionaries.

INDEX TO VERSES FREQUENTLY QUOTED BY CHRISTIAN MISSIONARIES